PLANNING RESEARCH FOR RESOURCE DECISIONS

CARL H. STOLTENBERG
RESEARCH ADMINISTRATOR / DEAN, SCHOOL OF FORESTRY,
OREGON STATE UNIVERSITY, CORVALLIS

KENNETH D. WARE
BIOMETRICIAN / ASSOCIATE PROFESSOR, DEPARTMENT OF
FORESTRY, IOWA STATE UNIVERSITY, AMES

ROBERT J. MARTY
RESOURCE ECONOMIST / ASSOCIATE PROFESSOR, DEPARTMENT OF FOREST
MANAGEMENT, MICHIGAN STATE UNIVERSITY, EAST LANSING

ROBERT D. WRAY
RESEARCH EDITOR / CHIEF, INFORMATION SERVICES, NORTH
CENTRAL FOREST EXPERIMENT STATION, FOREST SERVICE,
U.S. DEPARTMENT OF AGRICULTURE, ST. PAUL, MINNESOTA

J. D. WELLONS
WOOD CHEMIST / ASSOCIATE PROFESSOR, SCHOOL OF
FORESTRY, OREGON STATE UNIVERSITY, CORVALLIS

PLANNING
RESEARCH
FOR
RESOURCE
DECISIONS

THE IOWA STATE
UNIVERSITY
PRESS
AMES / IOWA

CONTENTS

v

PREFACE

This book defines a systematic approach to research on forest-resource problems. We believe this approach to planning is applicable to problem-oriented research in all the natural resources, but our experience and therefore our illustrations are built around problems in managing forests, wildlife, rangeland, watersheds, and outdoor recreation resources.

We emphasize planning and reporting because we feel that in the past these have been weak links in the research chain. Too many research programs are developed without the participants' agreeing upon a common basis for selecting and defining important problems, specifying the data needed to solve them, providing coordination of effort in obtaining these data, and assigning priorities among possible studies.

We are writing primarily for the neophyte resource researcher—the young scientist who is planning a resources research career. However, we hope the book will have broader use than this. Experienced investigators may find it contains materials for a good refresher course; perhaps it will be a source of new ideas. We see the resource manager—the ultimate user of research results—as a reader also; the better he understands the research process, the smaller will be the communications gap between research and management practices.

Poor planning frequently results in ineffective and fruitless research. Resources research demands intelligent and careful planning because forests and other natural communities are complex; they develop slowly over a long time and the economic and social impacts of changes in these communities are far reaching.

Research programs may be oriented around the various disciplines basic to forestry—biochemistry, soils, genetics, physiology, economics. Significant advantages could be cited for such an orientation to resources research, particularly in disciplinary departments of universities. Much of what we say in this book will be relevant and, we hope, helpful for research on problems defined by disciplinary criteria.

But the primary orientation for program planning in this book is not along disciplinary lines. Our presentation is based on what we feel to be the strong advantages of a decision-problem orientation for natural resources research. This orientation provides a workable and logical basis for selecting a definite, valuable objective for each study. It provides a framework for linking together all the studies needed to solve an important resource-related problem. Plans for these several studies can be synthesized into a coordinated master plan derived from a careful analysis of that problem.

Systematic research planning is easier when the results are quantitative and will be used immediately to help solve a resource manager's problem. But the added difficulties in planning qualitative or basic quantitative research do not make our problem orientation less useful. Instead they accentuate the need to focus on the resource manager's problem even though much time and several series of studies may be needed before the problem can be solved. In fact, research can contribute to efficient use of forest resources only if problems are anticipated years in advance so that the needed basic research can be completed before the problem actually develops.

The plan of the book parallels the decision-problem approach that we suggest for research planning. First, we define a model for understanding the relationship between resource management and research, and present the problem concept in this context. Bases for comparing problem priorities are discussed. Then, by considering one forest-resource problem and carefully analyzing it, we proceed through project planning to study planning and data recording and conclude with a discussion of how to report the results effectively. We try throughout the book to integrate the mechanics and philosophy of research, hoping to suggest the relationships between the *what,* the *why,* and the *how* of research methodology.

You will notice a gradual change in texture and scale from the first to the last chapters. In the early chapters, the broad subjects of program planning and problem analysis are treated in a general way. The young researcher needs to understand the research program context within which his study exists, but he is not likely to prepare the program plan. On the other hand, the chapters on study planning are more specific, although even here we treat in some detail only those topics of value to most natural resource researchers. For example, detailed measurement and instrumentation procedures for research in wood chemistry, limnology, ecology, and plant physiology are not covered; we give more attention to the basic considerations *behind* study objectives and statistical procedures. Finally, in the chapters on writing for publication we provide specific how-to-do-it suggestions, because the neophyte researcher needs these immediately.

The book concludes with an example of a project plan and a study plan, not submitted as models of perfection but rather as plans actually written by one scientist who used some of the ideas discussed in this book. As with most works, these exhibits illustrate some good planning—and some errors.

Throughout the book we have treated the subject matter in a way that is intended to be practical, helpful and, we hope, provocative. But in an effort to make it so, we may have erred on the side of brevity. Therefore, we have included references at the end of each chapter to provide sources of additional information on the subjects discussed.

ACKNOWLEDGEMENTS

The basic ideas and plans of this book were developed after extended discussions in 1962 between Carl Stoltenberg, Kenneth Ware, and Robert Marty, and

Allen Bickford, Professor, Department of Forest Management, New York College of Forestry at Syracuse University, Syracuse, New York,

Chester E. Jensen, Biometrician, Intermountain Forest Experiment Station, Ogden, Utah, and

Robert W. Wilson, Jr., U.S. Forest Service, Forest Insect and Disease Laboratory, West Haven, Connecticut.

Much of the final manuscript was the result of successive revisions, reorganizations, expansions, and deletions from the ideas and manuscripts initiated during those discussions.

We acknowledge also the contribution of graduate students at Iowa State University and Oregon State University, where several versions of the manuscript were used in courses in research methods. Their critical examination of the ideas and of our mode of presenting them has been helpful.

Constructive reviews, criticism, and comments from Henry J. Vaux, Carl E. Ostrom, Donald P. Duncan, John C. Gordon, Robert Buckman, and Henry H. Webster were particularly helpful in strengthening the final version.

PLANNING RESEARCH FOR RESOURCE DECISIONS

1

SCIENTISTS, RESEARCH, AND RESOURCE MANAGEMENT

Science is a manifestation of man's will to know and to understand both himself and the world around him. The process of scientific inquiry—of learning from nature—is a personal activity and one of the highest forms of creative endeavor. Rightly or wrongly, many a scientist feels he holds a special place in the world; that contemplation has great intrinsic value. This feeling does not depend on the practical result of his studies. Rather it stems from that infrequent moment when he comprehends what no one has comprehended before; when he perceives for the first time a new relationship, a new system, or a new order in his universe. The scientist is challenged by the unknown, and learning is his basic response to this challenge. To the scientist, then, the searching for knowledge of the natural world, like art and philosophy, offers a sense of participation in life that transcends normal experience. Science may be to the scientist not only an occupation or a means to some pragmatic end but also an end in itself. This much we take for granted.

But resource research should fit in with the rest of the world. Most of us are researchers because we like it, but all of us bear an important social responsibility as well. This responsibility to others is what makes science a profession, and it consists simply of choosing work that helps satisfy the wants of our fellowmen as well as our own personal desires (See, for example, Morison 1969). All new knowledge is useful, but some kinds are much more urgently needed by society than others. The first three chapters present a system for judging the practical significance of various types of research. We believe this a most important consideration for the scientist when

3

choosing what to study. Because of this consideration and because each scientist will normally undertake only a handful of major research efforts during his active career, each study should be chosen with care.

RESOURCES, RESOURCE MANAGERS, AND THEIR CLIENTS

In isolation, natural resources are valueless. They become valuable only when people are able to use them to satisfy human desires. Resources may be valuable to their owners for income, for raw material, or as a locale for recreation. Thus, forests are valuable to the logger or the sawmill owner because he wants the trees and logs to operate his business and to make his living. Rivers, lakes, and forests are valuable to the vacationer because he finds them desirable for his camping, fishing, and other recreational activities. Municipalities find some forests valuable because they protect the quality of their water supplies.

When many human wants can be satisfied more effectively by using forests and forest products than by using other localities or other products, then forests assume greater value. But when other commodities satisfy peoples' needs more efficiently, the importance of forests diminishes. This relationship is important because it clearly shows resource management to be a means to various ends rather than an end in itself. The relationship appropriately places the focus on the persons to be served and on the wants to be satisfied by resource management.

The critical importance of efficient management also becomes obvious. And it is indeed because efficiency is so important that we have resource managers. The ability of range managers to help satisfy human desires efficiently determines the proportion of capital and human resources that will be spent on range land rather than on beef feed-lot production which could also satisfy some of the same human desires. Similar examples could be offered for managers of watershed, wildlife, timber, and recreation resources.

Thus, as the forest resource manager learns new uses for his resource, he will be making a greater contribution to society. Simultaneously he will be making that resource more valuable and as he makes management operations more efficient, he will again be increasing his contribution to society.

In performing his professional activities, the resource manager assists his clients in four major ways (Stoltenberg *et al* 1961). First, he helps them identify and clarify their objectives. For example, the land manager may help identify the various personal satisfactions that the owner is seeking in managing his land. Second, the resource manager identifies for the client the various alternative ways of achieving the client's objectives. Third, he helps his client evaluate or compare these alternatives, *i.e.*, he helps him select the most promising or most efficient opportunities for achieving his objectives. And, fourth, the manager usually supervises the subsequent activities to implement these decisions. In other words, the natural-resource manager is a professional consultant who helps his client identify and solve resource problems.

Resource managers frequently spend such a large proportion of their time implementing decisions that insufficient emphasis is given to problem solving, that is, to the critically important phases leading to the decision to undertake particular activities. This is unfortunate because it is when he is helping his client to make decisions that the resource manager is often making his most valuable and typically professional contribution. Similarly, his greatest contributions in supervising management practices are made in the problem-solving or decision-making role.

RESEARCH, RESOURCE SCIENTISTS, AND THEIR CLIENTS

Natural-resource science and scientists are valuable to society for the same reasons that natural resources and their managers are valuable—they can help satisfy people's wants. And this is the main reason that society supports their research (Heady 1961; Dubos 1967). Just as the resource manager's contribution is measured by how effectively he helps others to satisfy their wants efficiently, the productive value of resource scientists must ultimately be determined by how much their efforts increase the efficiency of the resource manager.

This, then, provides the basis for a tentative statement about the purposes of natural-resources research. One major purpose is to develop new alternatives for the resource manager. These may be new practices, tools, and concepts, or new products and services. A second common purpose of resource research is to answer questions of fact that arise during management. And inasmuch as resource management is viewed as the process of solving clients' resource problems, these answers would be the information needed to solve these problems. That is, resource research provides the information needed to define or compare alternative means for achieving a resource user's or owner's objectives. A third purpose is to answer questions of fact that arise during resource research since it is only after some of these basic questions have been satisfactorily answered that the first two objectives can be achieved most efficiently.

Many resource researchers do not directly provide information for the resource manager. Some provide information to solve other researchers' problems. Resource research may be viewed as a continuous spectrum of scientists with the resource manager at one end of the spectrum. The manager is principally concerned with his client's problem, that of the resource owner or user. But when he lacks the information needed to help evaluate the client's alternative resource practices, he may experiment with several of those practices. Next on the spectrum are the scientists who are attempting to answer the managers' immediate questions of fact, such as resource-use trends, prices, and technologies. Following them are the developmental researchers who create new alternatives for the manager, particularly alternatives that will help solve problems not only of tomorrow but of years to come.

Further along this research spectrum are the scientists who serve a clientele of other researchers. These scientists, usually from the basic disciplines, provide the facts and relationships needed by other scientists who conduct the more "applied" developmental research. The relationship between applied and basic research is central to the history and philosophy of science and technology. Kranzberg (1967, 1968) discusses this briefly but comprehensively.

Although the ultimate client for all resource activities is the resource-manager's client, the immediate clientele of a researcher may be managers or other researchers. But every productive researcher has a clientele to whom he provides research results. This clientele uses his results to solve their resource-management, or research problems. When the client is another researcher, he in turn is able to conduct his research more efficiently and then provide his clientele with improved answers to help solve their resource-management research or practice problems.

As the distance on the spectrum increases between the manager and any researcher, successful problem anticipation, and hence planning, become more difficult. Although a scientist focuses primarily on his immediate client, his most basic research is really intended to help solve a resource-management problem. The research planner needs to anticipate that problem accurately. Thus researchers in the basic resource sciences are helping to solve important problems not expected to be critical for 5, 10, or even 20 years. This scientist may have great difficulty in anticipating the correct problem, but he is very valuable to society when he succeeds.

The results of some scientists' research will be useful in the solution of several clients' problems. This is particularly true for basic research. For example, a tree physiologist, a biochemist, and a wood anatomist might be teamed to study how trees form wood. Their results could help wood chemists develop pulping processes. But the same results could help organic chemists define the structure of lignin and likewise help forest biologists control tree growth. In turn, silviculture researchers can develop appropriate fertilization systems to satisfy the timber managers' needs.

Clearly, this research team may question the need for being concerned with which particular client's problem they are working on. In such instances, overemphasis on an ultimate problem (that of the resource manager's client) can result in confusion. In these situations, problem orientation can be achieved by having the silviculture researcher understand the biological-data needs in the probable decision-making framework of the timber manager and his potential clients; having the forest biologist understand the cultural needs in the decision-making framework of the silviculturist; having the physiologist understand the data and physical-relationship concerns of the biology researcher; and having each in turn respond to these needs.

Some researchers may feel that basic research is inherently nonproblem oriented. But we and many other researchers believe that a problem orientation both helps the researcher develop his research plans and enhances the value of even the most basic resource research (Balch 1964; Quinn and Cavanaugh 1964; Speith 1964; Hoover 1965).

COORDINATION AND EFFICIENT RESEARCH

The necessity (and difficulty) of coordinating the efforts of researchers is obvious if an efficient and successful attack on the problem is to be made. When several types of information are needed to solve a problem, failure to obtain just one bit of information may prevent solving the problem, and thus waste the research efforts invested in obtaining the other information. If communication and coordination are effective, managers will be continuously provided with better information to help their clients gain greater benefits from natural resources. With various degrees of success the needed coordination is achieved in several ways, a few of which will be mentioned to show the diversity of patterns that exist.

When a large amount of research effort can be concentrated on the solution of a particular problem, the problem itself may form the framework for a large research project. (We have provided an example of such a project plan in Chapter 12). The project in turn would be composed of closely coordinated individual studies designed to provide most of the facts or information required to solve the problem. Thus, if the problem deals with selecting the most efficient white pine weevil-control program for a forest pest-control agency, for example, individual studies might have forest entomologists investigating the flight patterns and other behavioral characteristics of the weevil; wood technologists estimating the effect of various weevil-attack frequencies on lumber-grade recovery from white pine trees; economists studying lumber or stumpage price trends and making treatment-cost studies; soils specialists defining the relationship of various soil conditions to site quality; and silviculturists defining the relationship of stand density to white pine growth rates on various sites. These efforts might be coordinated by a specific project plan that is designed, studied, and agreed upon by all of the researchers involved. Or coordination might be sought simply by developing exceptionally effective communication and close cooperation among the various researchers.

Close cooperation among researchers within the same discipline is also frequently required. For example, several entomologists might be working on different facets of the same problem, such as selecting a control method for an insect pest in recreation areas. One may be attempting to define different phases of an insect's life cycle. Another may be working on the effectiveness of various biological controls that might be used in regulating the insect. Each entomologist will contribute an important link of information that will be needed to solve the particular problem with which they all are concerned.

Thus, although the diversity in the techniques and forms of natural resources research is great, important relationships among researchers can be derived from the problem they are seeking to help solve. And because of these relationships there is a unifying pattern to the research activities as a whole.

So we see research activities gaining organization and orientation from: the flow of information needs and requests from managers outside of research; through education and extension specialists or applied researchers to the more applied studies; and finally to the more basic studies. Continuous communication between client and manager, practitioner and researcher, and among various kinds of researchers is necessary if research efforts are to be most effective.

Perhaps the weakest link in communication and understanding is that between researchers and managers. The manager often fails to communicate his information needs to researchers because he doesn't understand the type of information that research can provide; and researchers frequently don't seem to provide the information that is most urgently needed to help managers gain greater benefits from the resources for their clients—perhaps because researchers don't understand the client's objectives or their management alternatives. Unfortunately, increased specialization among researchers is likely to aggravate rather than solve this difficulty. For this reason, interest in strengthening the educational function that could bridge this gap is increasing, regardless of whether this function is to be performed by professors, extension foresters, applied researchers, articulate managers, or whomever (Macon 1967; Macon, Webster, and Hilliker 1969).

The reasons for poor communication between researchers and resource managers are not obscure. First of all, most resource scientists now are specialists, often working in the basic sciences rather than in applied forestry research. Most of these scientists orient primarily toward their scientific specialty and a clientele of other basic researchers rather than toward practical forestry problems. Unfortunately, this clientele of other researchers is also serving a clientele of basic scientists, thus forming a closed circle of communication, a circle that includes neither the applied scientist nor the resource manager. Then, too, the work of the basic scientist, because it is specialized, appears narrow to the manager. In fact, it has often, quite properly, no direct utility to managers. Because more and more researchers are orienting toward science rather than practice, and because, therefore, their contributions to knowledge may not have direct application to practice, improved communication between research and resource management must be established. The communications difficulty is an inevitable result of specialization in resource science and practice. Both scientists and managers must be aware of the difficulty and take pains to ameliorate it. Effective planning of research programs and projects will help.

To make sure that his research activities will be likely to form a logical pattern and, taken together with those of his fellow researchers, will constitute an effective attack on natural resource problems, the conscientious researcher will seek, first, to be continuously aware of the ultimate objectives of resource management (and thus of resource research); second, to visualize the logical flow of information from researcher, to researcher, to educator, to manager; and, third, to be receptive to a return flow of questions from manager, to researcher, to researcher.

Discussions with other researchers at scientific meetings and with resource managers at professional meetings and on the job (the manager's job) will help. Research advisory committees can help by discussing goals in long-range production and management with researchers. Problem-oriented research programs and project-planning conferences among researchers help improve communications too. Written reviews of project and study plan can contribute also. No one device will solve the communication problem among researchers and practitioners—but an awareness of the problem's existence and a series of efforts will reduce its impact.

REFERENCES

ACKOFF, R. L. 1962. Scientific method. Wiley, N. Y. 464 p.

BALCH, R. E. 1964. The future in forest entomology. J. of Forestry 62(1):11-18.

DUBOS, R. J. 1967. Scientists alone can't do the job. Saturday Review, (Dec. 2, 1967):68-71.

HEADY, E. O. 1961. Public purpose in agricultural research and education. J. Farm Econ. 43(3):566-581.

HOOVER, S. R. 1965. Research and purpose. In Letters to the Editor. Science 147:1523.

KRANZBERG, M. 1967. The unity of science-technology. Am. Scientist 55(1):48-66.

———. 1968. The disunity of science-technology. Am. Scientist 56(1):21-34.

MACON, J. W. 1967. On connections between research and forest management. J. Forestry 65(1):24-28.

MACON, J.W., H.H. WEBSTER, and R.L. HILLIKER. 1970. For more effective links between resource management and research. J. Forestry 68(2):84-86.

MORISON, R. S. 1969. Science and social attitudes. Science 165:150-156.

QUINN, J. B., and R. M. CAVANAUGH. 1964. Fundamental research can be planned. Harvard Bus. Rev. 42(1):111-124.

RASMUSSEN, L. W. 1964. Allocating resources in accomplishing research objectives. Agri. Sci. Rev. 2(1):24-30.

SIMON, H. 1960. The new science of management decision. Harper, N. Y. 50 p.

SPIETH, W. 1964. Basic research on a problem. In Letters to the Editor. Science 143:197.

STOLTENBERG, C. H., R. J. MARTY, and H. H. WEBSTER. 1961. Appraising forestry investment opportunities—the role of the investor, the forestry practitioner, and the researcher. In Proc. Soc. Am. Foresters (Washington, D.C., 1960):82-85.

WOLFGANG, R. 1965. Pure research, cultism, and the undergraduate. Science 150:1563-1565.

Research Program
Problem
Priority
Reduce air pollution, slash burning –
Seedling survival, SW counties – 2
Bark beetle control –
Blacktail deer harvest rate –
Increased bark utilization – 1
Recreation use –

2
PLANNING RESEARCH PROGRAMS

The research program of any organization is determined partly by pressures of clientele needs on researchers (individually and collectively) and partly by researchers' willingness to respond to them. In part, too, the research program is determined by available resources, which include the facilities and the personal talents and propensities of the organization's research staff. And in part the program will reflect the interests of those who provide the funds—members of a legislature, a board of directors, or a research foundation.

No one of these influencing elements is independent of the others. But because the number of potential problems is limitless and the resources to support research on them are limited, choices must be made. The productivity of various research activities differs widely, however, and is at least somewhat predictable. Thus, careful selection of research emphasis becomes not only fruitful but essential to maximum productivity.

Then, too, careful and considered planning will increase the productivity of research by assuring better coordination of research activities. Thus, responsible researchers plan their research programs carefully and seek to have these plans reviewed frequently by their clientele and by other researchers. National research programs, such as those cited in our reference list, are useful guides for the research planner.

The first step in research program planning is to specify the major problems on which research might be conducted; the second is to select for immediate attention those that have the highest priority.

SPECIFYING THE RESEARCHABLE PROBLEMS

In large research organizations, decisions on project and study emphasis will be made at various levels by the individual researcher, by the agency head, or by administrators in between. Effective communication among participating planners is therefore essential if the eventual program is to approach optimum effectiveness. Two of the greatest barriers to communication in research program planning have been failure to agree on (1) a consistent definition of what constitutes a researchable problem and (2) criteria to use in selecting those problems that should be studied first. The following definition and criteria have proved useful to the writers and will be used in the remaining sections of this text.

Problems are characteristic of people. A person has a problem of choice when he has alternate ways of achieving an objective and is in doubt about the most appropriate alternative. People have forest-resource problems when they are considering using forests or forest products to achieve their objectives, and when they seek to choose the most appropriate use or practice to achieve that objective. Specifically, a problem exists and is fully defined when the following are identified (Ackoff 1962):

1.*The decision-maker*—the client or client group who has the problem of choice. It may be landowners, the land manager, a wood-user group, or a group of researchers.

2. *The decision-maker's objective*—it may be maximum dollar income, obtaining the greatest satisfaction in the form of recreation from a specific cash outlay, estimating stand growth rates, predicting future water yields, or comparing the photosynthetic efficiency of species.

3. *Alternatives*—at least two unequally efficient courses of action that have some chance of yielding the desired objective. This could be increased pen raising and release vs. direct habitat improvement to increase a wildlife population, or platen drying vs. convection drying of hardwood veneer. In estimating timber growth, the available alternatives might include use of yield tables, local average growth estimates, or a regression equation developed from remeasured-plot data.

4. *Doubt*—as to which choice is best.

5. *An environment*–the context of the problem, external or uncontrolled factors that affect the solution.

The application of this problem concept in research, its usefulness and its limitations, are considered in greater detail in Chapter 3.

If we accept this definition, the question of how to determine which problems have the highest priority for research attention still remains. Both the problem concept and the selection criteria can be illustrated by considering research program formulation to be a problem in these terms.

In this illustration the decision-maker could be the individual researcher, the project leader, the agency head, or whoever is concerned with choosing among research problems for study.

The general objective of the decision-maker might be to specify a research program that will supply information and the product-process developments that will contribute most at a given cost toward helping his clientele use forests and forest products to achieve their objectives more efficiently. But such a general objective must be modified to fit the specific situation of any individual research decision-maker. For example, in a university, the training of graduate students in research methods may be a major consideration; then the objective might be modified to indicate that the research program must be one that can be carried out in part by graduate students working under the supervision of their professors. Or if the decision-maker were a specialist in wildlife biology, he might modify the objective by considering only those programs in which the major research required would be biological. And if the decision-maker's responsibilities were regional (or single-company), the objectives would, of course, be modified accordingly.

So much for the researcher's objective. But what then are his alternatives—the different programs that might be followed to achieve that objective?

First to be considered in listing potential research problems is the clientele to be served and not the specific talents of the research staff. This is necessary if the ultimate focus of forest-resource research is to be on helping people to obtain greater benefits from forests and forest products.

After selecting the clientele, the next step is to anticipate important future problems of that group and analyze these problems to determine the general type of studies needed to solve each one. For example, the primary clientele group for a carbohydrate chemist in a forest products laboratory might be the paper technologists of the region's pulp and paper industry. Among the problems these technologists might be seeking to solve are selecting the best cooking process to make a specific grade of pulp, identifying the most practical way of strengthening the paper currently being produced, and deciding whether hardwood chips or softwood sawdust will provide the best source of fiber for expanding production. The type of studies needed to solve each problem would, of course, differ.

The resulting list of potential problems is likely to be too long for a single research program, but some problems can be deleted rather quickly by considering the talents and inclinations of the research staff. Some forest-resource scientists want to provide data for immediate solution of the resource manager's problem. These scientists may provide some answers by compiling facts from experience and research literature and combining these with personal judgment and perhaps the results of observations or brief investigations. In universities, such research might be designed by forest-management researchers, other applied-research persons, or by qualified extension specialists. The point is that this is one very useful form of forestry research.

But as the potential research problems are analyzed and the immediate-use data synthesized, it will be apparent that some estimates are unreliable or highly speculative. The need to test the validity of some hypotheses will be obvious also. In spite of the recognized need for such additional research, the researcher who analyzed the problem and developed the initial estimates may not be able to proceed to the additional studies. His interests, time limitations, and lack of know-how or resources may prevent his doing this research himself. If communication is good among researchers, others will be aware of these *researcher* problems and will consider them as alternatives for *their* research.

For example, the first researcher in the spectrum might provide estimates of the future yield needed to solve the resource manager's problem by assuming that the relationship between site and the stand growth is adequately defined by yield tables based on species, site index, and age, and by assuming also that yield is directly proportional to stocking (stand density), expressed in percent of normal basal area. However, is basal area the best measure of stocking? Is the relationship between stocking and growth really linear? Would some combination of soil characteristics be associated more closely with growth than is site index? The problem analysis may reveal that answers to these questions will be needed in the future. Reliable solutions for these researcher problems depend on facts that must be provided by more basic research, much of which can be conducted more efficiently by other researchers.

The point is that some researchers and even some research groups are better equipped for conducting basic research on the problems of other researchers, whereas some researchers can work more effectively on problems of resource managers. Early recognition of this fact and correct identification of one's clientele will save much effort in defining the research program alternatives, *i.e.*, in "specifying the problems" for possible inclusion in a research program.

ASSIGNING RESEARCH PRIORITIES

After the available financial, human, and other resources have been considered and the relevant research problems specified, the other major phase of research program formulation is assigning priorities to the problems. Or, in the problem context that we have been using, the final step is to compare the research program alternatives and to assign priorities to them according to appropriate criteria.

Although many things may influence research priorities, timing should be one of the most important. The results of experimental research planned today are not likely to have much bearing on the solution of the managers' current problems. Research, together with management, must try to define the problems of tomorrow and program planning should focus on providing well-defined alternatives and useful criteria for solving these projected problems. The long time span from research to practice makes this approach admittedly risky, but absolutely necessary if absurdities are to be avoided. Basic research must be designed to apply to a broader range of more distant problems than applied research. The analysis of such distant problems will contain many uncertainties, but it need be no less rigorous than the manager's analysis of today's problems. Research that solves yesterday's problems only, or that is merely curiosity seeking, should be eliminated from the priority list.

Quantitative estimates of research's anticipated value are helpful in setting program priorities, but they do not replace the much-needed judgment of the program planner. Program planning and budgeting systems (PPBS) are a first attempt to provide a systematic basis for allocating research effort in governmental programs (McKean 1958; Novick 1966). Similar systems are also used in private institutional and industrial research planning (Sandretto 1968). Kaldor (1966) dealt with a systematic approach to setting priorities for research in the agricultural experiment stations.

These systems generally are based on the ratio of the social or economic benefits of a study and the estimated costs of the research. The benefit-cost ratio is usually weighted according to the probability of the research meeting its objectives. Many methods have been used to estimate research benefits. Bethune and Clutter (1969), for example, suggest using stand-growth models to evaluate research on forest management. They calculated the effect on yield of varying the type and intensity of certain management practices. By estimating the relative costs of the research needed to bring about those levels of management, they were able to obtain benefit-cost estimates for each type of research. These then were subjected to analysis based on dynamic programming to determine optimum distribution expenditures.

In spite of the difficulty of assigning dollar values to research accomplishments, particularly for qualitative research in public resource policy, recreation resources, and other social science areas of natural-resource management, most organizations have concluded that some system for evaluating program alternatives objectively is better than purely subjective selection.

Although quantitative comparisons are not always possible, answers to the following questions may help in achieving a ranking of the probable contributions of research to solving the selected problems.

Benefit considerations:

1. How many decision-makers (managers or researchers) have this problem? Will the problem be more important in the future?

2. How inadequate is the information currently being used to solve it? Are the clients possibly making wrong decisions now? If so, how costly might such wrong decisions be? How soon can better information be provided?

3. Would the answers that we obtain be used? Or is additional information needed?

4. Will the answers be useful for solving other problems?

5. Comparing the resources of other research groups with our own, do we have any unusual research capabilities that would enable us to be more effective than other groups in conducting research on

certain kinds of problems? Resources such as:
personnel (exceptional senior scientists or number of graduate assistants),
collaborative groups,
facilities and locations, or
client contracts.
Cost considerations:

1. What financing will be required? (Do we have it? Can we get it?)

2. What other research resources are required? (Do we have them? Can we get them?)

ASSIGNING PRIORITIES FOR NONPROBLEM-ORIENTED RESEARCH

The problem of deciding which research should receive available research resources (time, talents, equipment, and dollars) is not resolved by disclaiming any interest in problem-oriented research. Because the number of possible studies is limitless and research resources are always limited, decisions must be made about which studies to conduct and how to conduct them. Every researcher must make these decisions, although his objectives and alternatives and the context of his decisions will differ from those of other researchers. All too often these crucial choices have been made by default.

Some scientists claim their efforts would be most productive if they simply "followed their interests." For the experienced and successful research worker this may well be true. But if so, it is because he has already established close and successful communication with his clientele and is familiar with their problems and the kinds of information they need. (It is of course not at all important whether he refers to these incentives as "clientele, problems, and information needs" or by some other terms.)

Thus, even if a scientist has Thoreau-like austerity and isolation, singleness of purpose, and an independent source of income and support, he still must choose what studies to conduct and which of these to conduct first. Let's assume this scientist considers himself to be his own client in seeking knowledge for knowledge's own sake and for personal satisfaction. Would it not be sensible for him to consider, just as the problem solver would, which studies should be done first and how they should be done so that he might advance knowledge further in the time available, and thus gain greater personal satisfaction?

The successful researcher undoubtedly has in the back of his mind a sufficient number of studies to more than fill his lifetime. He has also considered what would be the most efficient use of his own time in conducting these studies, and he has reached decisions either by plan or default. The question now is not whether to assign priorities and choose among study techniques, but what basis to use in so doing. The experienced researcher combines a sixth sense with some more formal method of problem analysis and study planning.

The neophyte researcher, on the other hand, does not yet have any such subconscious knowledge or any rapport with a clientele. Nor is he likely to be given an opportunity to "follow his interest." For him, a formal problem-oriented approach to research planning would help greatly in making the unavoidable decisions about which specific study objective to select and which procedures to use in conducting the study to achieve that objective.

Without some rational basis for making decisions, the graduate student or novice researcher will make these inevitable choices on the basis of expediency: *i.e.*, what he thinks his dissertation committee will accept as "scholarly"; what his major professor's (or project leader's) last graduate student did when he was working on such a study (as recorded in the library copy of his thesis); or what fits most conveniently into his class schedule and available research time. When research decisions continually are made in this way, the educational value of the student's research experience is threatened. Perhaps funding sources will eventually find other places to invest their money under greater promise of returns in both research and research training.

REFERENCES

ACKOFF, R. L. 1962. Scientific method. Wiley, N. Y. 464 p.

BETHUNE, J. E., and J. L. CLUTTER. 1969. Allocating funds to timber management research. Forest Sci. Monograph 16. 22 p.

CHARTRAND, R. L. 1968. Congress seeks a systems approach. Datamation 14(5):46-49.

GREENBERG, D. S. 1967. The politics of pure science. Saturday Review (Nov. 4, 1967):62-68.

KALDOR, D. R. 1966. A framework for establishing research priorities. J. Farm Econ. 48(5):1629-1640.

LIPETZ, B. 1965. The measurement of efficiency of scientific research. Intermedia, Carlisle, Mass. 262 p.

LLOYD, L. E. 1966. Techniques for efficient research. Chemical Pub. Co., New York. 215 p.

MARSHAK, R. E. 1966. Basic research in the university and industrial laboratory. Science 154:1521-1524.

MCKEAN, R. N. 1958. Efficiency in government through systems analysis, with emphasis on water resources development. Wiley, New York. 336 p.

NOVICK, D., ed. 1967. Program budgeting. Harvard Univ. Press, Cambridge, Mass. 382 p. (Abridged version available from U.S. Government Printing Office.)

PELZ, D. C. 1967. Creative tensions in the research and development climate. Science 157:160-165.

PRICE, D. K. 1966. Federal money and university research. Science 151:285-290.

SANDRETTO, P. C. 1968. The economic management of research and engineering. Wiley, N.Y. 199 p.

SHICK, A. 1966. The road to PPB: the stages of budget reform. Public Admin. Rev. 26(4):243-258.

U.S. DEPT. AGRI. and STATE AGRI. EXP. STA. TASK FORCE. 1966. A national program of research for agriculture. USDA, Coop. State Res. Serv., Wash., D.C. 272 p.

———. 1967. A national program of research for forestry. USDA, Coop. State Res. Serv., Wash., D.C. 73 p.

U.S. FOREST SERVICE. 1964. A national forestry research program. USDA Misc. Publ. 965. 34 p.

WESTVELD, R. H., and F. H. KAUFERT. 1964. Progress in activating the McIntire-Stennis Act. J. Forestry 62(7):451-455.

WOLFE, E., ed. 1959. Symposium on basic research. Publ. 56, Am. Assn. Adv. Sci., Washington, D.C. 308 p.

YOVITS, M. C., D. M. GILFORD, R. H. WILCOX, E. STAVELEY, and H. D. LERNER. 1966. Research program effectiveness. Gordon and Breach, Science Publishers, New York. 542 p.

3
PROBLEM ANALYSIS
AND PROJECT PLANNING

In this and the remaining chapters we shall be concerned with how you as an individual researcher may apply scientific methods—first, in analyzing resource problems and then in designing studies to provide some of the data needed to solve these problems.

Three steps are appropriate in problem analysis and project planning before specific study planning. First, the analyst specifies the problem clearly. Second, he identifies the facts, relationships, or models that must be known to solve the problem and describes how these can indeed be combined to solve the problem. And third, selecting all or several of the related facts, relationships, or models that are to be derived from individual research studies, he outlines a research project that identifies the studies and shows their interrelationships. Before considering these three steps in detail, we need to define our concept of projects and studies. By research *project* we mean a group of individual studies meant to supply the information needed to solve a specific resource problem. We begin by identifying a problem in public policy or private resource management, then determine what kinds of information are needed to solve it. These information needs define the objectives of the individual studies that will make up the project.

Our concept differs from the common one in which research projects are groups of studies based on similar scientific subject matter (plant physiology, economics, pathology, and so forth). And our concept differs also from the one in which studies are grouped by the resource they are intended to serve (range or timber type, plant or animal species). These systems of organizing research have their place;

ours has a special purpose. Problem-oriented projects are meant to create a bridge between the scientific research organization and the clientele of researchers, resource managers, and policy makers.

Because the project focuses on the problem of interest, the project may be aimed at a policy issue or a management question, an area of scientific interest, or some other problem. But, since the study is designed to provide a specific item of information, it may be more neutral in problem content. As an example, a recent project was aimed at identifying the opportunities for intensifying timber management in the National Forests (Marty and Newman 1969) and resulted in a specific public-program recommendation. One group of studies within this project developed estimates of the relative efficiency of intensified timber management on different timber types, sites, and geographic locations, by estimating yield increments, management cost increases, and unit product values for each timberland class. Other studies were needed to define the extent of current opportunities for intensification in each class. None of these studies had any policy implications in itself, and some of them will even be useful in guiding private management of these timber types as well as public forest policy.

STEP 1: SPECIFY THE PROBLEM

Rarely will you, as a researcher, be handed a detailed plan for a study. To develop such a plan, your first step is to understand clearly the problem to be solved and define it. Only by understanding your clientele's problem, and how your intended results will be used to solve it, will you have an adequate basis for deciding: What facts, relationships, models are needed? In what form would they be most useful? What precision is needed? What population should be sampled?

A problem will be fully specified when clear answers are provided to four questions: (a) Who is the decision-maker? (b) What is his objective? (c) What are his most promising alternative courses of action? (d) What is the problem context?

(a) *Who is the decision-maker?* Occasionally, research will be conducted to solve a single individual's problem, but this is the exception. Usually the problem will be one shared by many people, companies, agencies, or research groups if it is to merit consideration for major research support. Therefore the decision-maker will usually be a composite of people who have a particular problem in common. This group then should be identified and described.

(b) *What is his objective?* Although this is a simple question, you may find it hard to answer. Frequently, decision-makers are not able to state their objectives clearly. In fact, as we said in Chapter 1, a major function of resource managers is to help decision-makers clarify their objectives.

If the decision-maker's objectives were adequately specified, the resource manager could identify alternative means of achieving them and then choose the most appropriate alternative without again consulting the decision-maker. But rarely is this possible. Usually the stated objective serves as a tentative basis for selection only. It enables the manager to suggest practices and to make a tentative selection that may be modified by the decision-maker on the basis of other unquantifiable or as-yet-unspecified facets of his objectives.

Because the decision-maker may be a composite of a group, the researcher may have to specify objectives that would not exactly suit any single decision-maker, but would be generally acceptable by the entire group.

(c) *What are the most promising alternatives?* What different means does the decision-maker have for achieving his objective? For timberland owners, for example, these alternatives may be specific forestry practices such as thinning, fertilization, planting; they may be different intensities of applying a given practice; or they may be various stands in which a practice might be applied. If a researcher is trying to find the best way to measure water yield in a study of watershed-vegetation manipulation, for example, the alternatives he might consider could include total runoff, or runoff plus water table recharge, and might be measured at the weir or at a downstream point of use. In any case, the researcher must specify the most relevant alternatives in light of the decision-maker's objectives.

(d) *What is the problem context (environment)?* What factors affect the relationship between the alternatives proposed and the degree to which they satisfy the objective? What are the circumstances that must be known and accounted for to derive the optimum solution? There will be circumstances that the decision-maker cannot control, or doesn't wish to change, but which influence how well his objective can be achieved by each of the alternatives. For example, his decision might be limited by the kinds of stands that are currently owned, the kinds of equipment that are available or can be acquired, or the market outlets in a specific area. By identifying the problem context, you will have completed Step 1—you will have specified the problem.

STEP 2: IDENTIFY THE FACTS, RELATIONSHIPS, OR MODELS NEEDED TO SOLVE THE PROBLEM

After clearly stating the problem, the analysis is concluded by describing how to solve it. To do this, you must describe the criteria that you think the decision-maker will use in comparing his alternatives, and specify the data needed to apply these criteria.

Some of these data will be relations, such as those between soil characteristics and plant growth. Others will be specific facts, such as the size of a fish population, or the value of an animal-month of forage. The data may be obtained directly from research, or may be estimated from models developed by research. These data needs then may become the objectives for applied research and, because the applied research is based on more fundamental facts and relationships, the data needs give a problem orientation to more basic research as well.

A simplified outline of two sample problems and the facts, relations, or models needed to solve them might be helpful in understanding these points. Assume the decision-makers are private individuals who own cutover land in western Oregon. This land has not reseeded naturally. The objective of these landowners is "to maximize economic returns from growing timber on this land with an added investment not to exceed $50 per acre." The alternatives include various seeding and planting practices, and future stand-management procedures. But for this example, we shall consider only the various kinds of regeneration practices. They include age and treatment of planting stock, species, seed source, and seedling spacing. The context includes planting sites, equipment, and competing vegetation. A criterion or decision rule is needed to choose among these alternatives: our decision-makers wish to know which reforestation method will provide the greatest net present worth when costs and returns are discounted at 6 percent.

To solve this problem we need estimates of future markets and product prices; the estimates of the relationship between seed source and seedling spacing and stand volumes at various ages for various sites and thinning schedule; seedling and planting costs for various spacings; and so on. Thus we have identified the problem, the decision rule, and then the facts and relationships needed to choose among the alternative solutions.

As a second example, assume that researchers are trying to develop new wood-preservation processes. At present, the oils and oil carriers used for the more permanent treatments make the wood surface unpaintable. The objective might be "to develop a process for treating posts and poles that will cost less than $3 per cubic foot, but will allow the posts and poles to be painted." Among the available alternatives might be impregnating the wood with one of several preservative salts using gaseous or liquid carriers that don't interfere with exterior paint, applying water-soluble preservatives that can be chemically bound to the wood once impregnated, or developing new paints. The context might require that existing staff be used, which would eliminate developing a new paint as an alternative, that the process be "in line" within one year, or that existing production facilities be usable with minor modifications. The decision rule may specify selecting the alternative that will result in maximum profit for ten years with development costs not to exceed $200 thousand.

To make this decision many facts and relationships are needed. In addition to market and cost information, the decision-makers need to know the relations between toxicity and preservative penetration, between rate of preservative penetration and temperature, and between pressure and carrier viscosity.

STEP 3: OUTLINE A RESEARCH PROJECT

The problem analysis is now complete; the problem has been defined and the information needed to solve it has been specified. The needed information will usually include several relationships and facts. Some of these will be provided by the decision-maker,and some by his advisor, the resource manager or scientist. Where such existing information is unreliable, research may be needed to provide better estimates or models and thus more reliable solutions.

Of course when a decision will not wait for better information, resource managers and researchers must act on the best information available, sometimes making poor decisions and sometimes good ones. But research can be designed to provide data that will improve the "batting average."

Several studies will usually be required to solve a problem, because rarely is there one weak segment only in the problem-solving chain. Thus, in the preceding example, research might be conducted simultaneously to provide improved estimates of the effect of spacing on tree size, stand volume, and growth; the effect of planting stock phenotype on survival and early growth rate; and the effect of seed source on growth.

Even when only one fact or relation appears to need strengthening, several studies may be required. Better background knowledge is usually prerequisite to providing more reliable information for problem-solving. And, as outlined in Chapter 1, these underlying facts, relations, and models must come usually from rather specialized and basic (even though problem-oriented) research of other resource scientists. A key decision in research organization and planning is how best to assure an efficient, balanced, and coordinated series of studies to provide both the underlying knowledge and the improved problem-solving information. A balanced and efficient attack is not likely to emerge from scientists in several disciplines working independently on different aspects of the same problem. Each may be conducting two or three studies that will contribute—but how will the results tie together? How can we decide which information might be most useful in solving the client's problem?

A coordinated research effort can be provided if the scientists involved anticipate the problem and the decision rule used for its solution; observe particularly the relationships that need strengthening; and then identify the specific studies they might conduct independently and collectively. An outline of such a group of studies, or more frequently the facts and relationships these studies would provide, would constitute a research project outline.

Such project outlines can be written and formal, or they can be informal and exist only in the minds of the research team. The appropriate level of formality depends much upon the personnel involved—the research scientists themselves—how closely they work together, and how well they are able to keep in mind the ultimate problem they are seeking to solve. Written project outlines can be prepared by a project, team, or group leader, with various degrees of review and revision by the participating research scientists. Or, such outlines can be prepared as a synthesis of the study plans of the individual participants. The important point is that there be an awareness of the linkage between the various studies and of the interdependence of the studies.

Research project plans should be reviewed and revised frequently to assure continued pertinence. For some kinds of research, this will mean reviews every few months—for others, intervals as long as five years may be appropriate.

We cannot overemphasize project planning. It is the project plan which defines the relationship and provides the coordinating link between natural resources research of entomologists, pathologists, tree physiologists, wildlife biologists, economists, soil scientists, wood scientists, marketing specialists, hydrologists, and others. Unless projects are planned, many independent studies can be conducted without helping solve the problem. Or at least the problem may be solved only haphazardly and at a higher cost (Sherwin and Isenson 1967).

But formal structuring of research projects has its dangers, too. Most notable among these is the possibility of stifling the development and use of new ideas as the research is being conducted; researchers may erroneously consider the project outline to be a contract, rather than a revisable plan. Sufficient opportunity must always be provided for initiative and creativity by the participating scientists.

When several studies are linked to form a large research project, a formal system may be needed to evaluate the project's likely effectiveness. Operations research has led to a number of such systems. The Critical Path Method (CPM) is applied to planning, scheduling, and cost-control aspects of project work. Program Evaluation and Review Technique (PERT) is used for schedule evaluation in research projects to assess the probability of meeting deadlines and to identify likely bottlenecks in the schedule. These techniques are based on a charting of the project, *i.e.*, drawing a network that describes the flow of information from one study to another and finally to the decision-maker. The charting process in itself clarifies the interrelationships between the various studies and clearly identifies the communication channels both to the user of research results and from the user to the research groups. It can also be used to evaluate increases in project efficiency that result from changing the project outline to include new ideas. Details of these systems may be obtained in Hillier and Lieberman (1967).

A careful problem analysis and a related project plan is exceedingly helpful to you as an individual research scientist. The more you know about the problems you are working on and thus how your study results will be used, the more efficiently you will be able to conduct your research, whether basic or applied. In addition to telling you what data are needed and relevant, the problem-solving framework will also indicate the most useful form for your data (broad classification vs. continuous relationships, qualitative vs. quantitative, etc.); the precision that is required and perhaps the value of additional precision; and where your results should be published to be seen by the relevant audience.

PROBLEM MODIFICATION AS RESEARCH

Not all research is aimed at problem solving. In fact, a decision-maker frequently has no problem in the sense that no alternative course of action allows him to meet his objectives. Thus a major function of research is to create new alternatives, or to improve existing alternatives, and thus allow the decision-maker to more nearly satisfy his true objectives. These alternatives may be new products, new tools, new practices, new services, or new processes involving industrial equipment, computer programs, and mathematical equations. The research so frequently categorized as "developmental" or "engineering" research deals entirely with creating alternatives or improving existing ones.

The relationship of developmental research to problem analysis differs slightly from that described in the preceding section. When the objective is developmental, thorough problem analysis is critical, as before, because from it comes the specifications for whatever is being developed. But, unlike research to quantify relationships, the developmental problem analysis gives limited assistance in delineating study procedures (Gideonse 1968). Systematic planning can only establish the "sideboards" or focus for new developments—the rest must come from the scientist's own creativity. And although creative thinking can be enhanced by good planning, it can not be prescribed by formula. Parnes and Harding (1962) and Lloyd (1966) have discussed creativity and its role in research and development in detail. Project plans for developmental research are needed for the same reasons cited previously.

PROBLEM ANALYSIS AS RESEARCH

We have just described problem analysis as a rather formal process that precedes study planning. Its primary goal is the identification of specific information needs. The problem analysis thus becomes the basis for formulating project plans and study objectives.

Most researchers go through many of these problem-analysis steps subconsciously. By failing, however, to clearly identify the clientele's objectives and alternatives, or some other aspect of the problem, they frequently select poorer study objectives or less efficient study procedures than they might have otherwise. Sometimes this is unavoidable because the researcher is geographically separated from his clientele. Sometimes it is because a specific study must be begun immediately, without time for a careful problem analysis. Usually, however, it is omitted simply because researchers don't see how useful a more formal analysis could be.

Actually, conducting such problem analyses is a legitimate form of research in itself—although one not consciously and commonly practiced by many researchers. Much past resource research would have provided, with only slight modification, very effective problem analyses—and would have been more useful as a result. Numerous forest-ownership studies can be cited as examples (James *et al.* 1951) (Yoho *et al.* 1957). Many of the land-use studies of the thirties summarized so effectively by Salter (1948), were of a similar nature—not research to test hypotheses or to carefully define relationships, but more to describe aspects of the context within which decisions were being made. Unfortunately, these studies did not always identify *whose* problems were being analyzed—the private resources owner's, or those of some public agency. As a result, many such analyses did not adequately identify the alternative courses of action, and thus did not describe specific data needs that would help the decision-makers choose among such alternatives. But surveys of decision-makers are one way of developing the basis for problem analyses—and a good way, if done with the objectives clearly in mind.

Case studies may help formulate a problem analysis, too, particularly when the clientele are faced with similar problems. For example, many resource managers are engaged in inventory work, and so must determine a sampling plan, select quantity and quality measures, specify field-crew organizations, and so forth. Perhaps carefully describing the decision framework used by one or two of these managers might provide helpful insights and an acceptable basis for an analysis of these problems.

A careful review of the literature, plus consultation with the decision-makers involved, is perhaps the commonest method of obtaining information for a problem analysis. This is because *most* forest resource research is rather fundamental and thus is aimed at a clientele of other researchers. Even if all resource research were problem oriented, research that would yield results directly usable by the manager would be a small fraction of the total research effort. But such research is the payoff end of a chain of coordinated research, from society's point of view.

Frequently a researcher will use his own research results as a basis for more applied research. When he does so, he is a part of his own clientele and, therefore should have a very good idea of what the problem is. In such cases, only a review of additional literature and some careful thinking are required to state the problem clearly, to make sure that it applies to a reasonably wide range of users, and to decide whether the data needs as specified are appropriate.

Whenever possible, problem analyses should, of course, be reviewed by selected clientele to make sure the analyst clearly understands the problem. For example, in studying the effect of various environmental factors on tree growth under controlled conditions, some method might be needed for measuring rates of photosynthesis. In turn, this would require the researcher to select the units in which he will measure the photosynthetic tissue of the tree seedling, one of the input units. Some researchers have chosen dry weight of needles, others total length of needles, others crown volume. Each variable gives a somewhat different result (Gordon and Gatherum 1967), but each researcher analyzes this problem and chooses among these various measures when he conducts this research. But before proceeding with his research, he should see whether his views coincide with those of others faced with the same problem.

As a final justification, problem analysis and project planning are becoming essential steps in gaining support for scientific work. In government the concepts of program budgeting are being applied to research just as they are to other expenditures. And private support, too, increasingly depends on ability to demonstrate the practical significance of the work. It is important for the scientist to understand that legislators and foundation heads view research as a means of accomplishing some public or social good, and not as an end in itself. Research is always in competition with other forms of expenditure—other kinds of investment.

REFERENCES

GIDEONSE, H. D. 1968. Research, development, and the improvement of education. Science 162:541-545.

GORDON, J. D., and G. E. GATHERUM. 1967. Correlations among fresh weight, dry weight, volume and total length of needles of Scotch pine seedlings. Forest Sci. 13:426-427.

HILLIER, F. S., and G. J. LIEBERMAN. 1967. Introduction to operation research. Holden-Day, San Francisco. 639 p.

JAMES, L. M., W. P. HOFFMAN, and M. A. PAYNE. 1951. Private forest land ownership and management in central Mississippi. Miss. State Coll. Agri. Exp. Sta. Tech. Bull. 33. 38 p.

LLOYD, L. E. 1966. Techniques for Efficient Research. Chemical Pub. Co., New York. 215 p.

MARTY, R. J., and W. NEWMAN. 1969. Opportunities for timber management intensification on the National Forests. J. Forestry 67(7):482-485.

PARNES, S.J., and H.F. HARDING. 1962. A source book for creative thinking. Scribner, New York. 393 p.

SALTER, L.A., Jr. 1948. A critical review of research in land economics. Univ. of Minnesota Press, Minneapolis, Minn. 258 p. (reissued in 1967, Univ. of Wisconsin Press)

SHERWIN, C. W., and R. S. ISENSON. 1967. Project hindsight: a defense department study of the utility research. Science 156:1571-1577.

YOHO, J. G., L. M. JAMES, and D. N. QUINNEY. 1957. Private forest land ownership and management in the northern half of Michigan's Lower Peninsula. Mich. State Univ. Agri. Exp. Sta. Tech. Bull. 261. 56 p.

4

SCIENTIFIC METHODS
AND MODELS

Before discussing further the planning, conduct, and reporting of research, it is appropriate to relate our discussions to the literature on science and scientific methods and to consider rather specifically the role of models in research.

We use the term science to allude to a body of facts and hypotheses about the natural world, the accumulated knowledge about natural objects and events. Scientific methods are those procedures by which facts and hypotheses are accumulated. They are procedures for learning and for organizing experience and generalizing upon it.

Scientific methods are rewarding because they introduce logic and objectivity into our attempts to describe and understand the world around us. Scientific methods embrace many specific learning techniques, all of which have several things in common. First, they prevent our interjecting personal bias into our observations and conclusions. Second, they force us to use systems of logic acceptable to all rational individuals. Because of the logical and objective nature of scientific inquiry, scientific findings tend to be accepted and used by persons other than those who developed them.

OBSERVATION AND HYPOTHESIS FORMULATION

The many specific learning techniques that form scientific methods can be divided into two basic categories: observation and hypothesis formulation.

Simply by observing a group of objects or events and reflecting on these observations, scientists have found it possible to discern stable patterns or relationships that seem to hold for the entire group. For instance, observation and reflection seem to have been Charles Darwin's basic method of learning. In the introduction to *Origin of Species* Darwin wrote:

"When on board the H.M.S. Beagle as naturalist, I was much struck with certain facts in the distribution of the organic beings inhabiting South America... These facts...seemed to throw some light on the origin of species—that mystery of mysteries, as it has been called by one of our greatest philosophers. On my return home, it occurred to me...that something might perhaps be made out by patiently accumulating and reflecting on all sorts of facts which could possibly have any bearing.... After five years work I allowed myself to speculate on the subject....."[1]

In this approach to learning, the scientist depends on repeated observations interspersed with studied reflection to disclose common attributes from which he postulates those general laws and unifying relationships that are the business of science.

In hypothesis formulation, the scientist seeks a unifying concept of a known body of facts, not by further observation, but rather by introspection and imagination. He attempts to arrange already known facts in a logical framework that explains what has been observed.

For instance, Nicolas Copernicus, in speaking of his revolutionary concept that the sun—rather than the earth—is the center of planetary movement, wrote:

"...I decided to try whether, on the assumption of some motion of the Earth, better explanations of the revolutions of the heavenly spheres might not be found..... I have found that when the motion of the other planets are referred to the circulation of the Earth, and are computed for the revolution of each star, not only do the phenomena necessarily follow therefrom, but also that the order and magnitude of the stars and of all their orbits...are so connected that in no part can anything be transposed without confusion to the rest....."[2]

Copernicus learned by seeking better explanations of facts already known. We reformulate our way of looking at phenomena, we alter our assumptions about the relationships among occurrences, and

---

[1] Darwin, Charles. 1859. Introduction to The Origin of species by means of natural selection or the preservation of favored races in the struggle for life. New American Library, New York Mentor Edition, 1958.

[2] Copernicus, Nicolas. 1543. *De Revolutionibus*. As reported by Singer, Charles. 1959. A short history of scientific ideas to 1900. Oxford Univ. Press, London. p. 213.

perhaps we arrive at a more logical and revealing conception of them. The reformation of hypotheses has lead to knowledge that might never be available from repeated observation alone.

The distinction drawn here between observation and hypothesis formulation is, of course, artificial. Scientific methods really require both. And learning proceeds best when both are fully employed.

It is interesting to note, however, that radical shifts in emphasis have taken place during the development of science. The scholastics of the middle ages almost completely disavowed observation as relevant in attempting an explanation of the physical world. Largely as a protest against the pragmatically unsatisfying results of the scholastic tradition, Francis Bacon suggested that scientists use observation as well as intuition and logic in seeking scientific knowledge.

We can note, even today, that some fields of inquiry emphasize the observational phase and others the hypothesis-formulation phase of scientific methods. For instance, in most biological research great dependence is placed on observation. You have often heard the maxim: "Know your organism!" This attitude probably has arisen because the objects of biological research are more readily available for study than those in many other fields. Observation is an obvious and natural course.

In the physical sciences, on the other hand, where the subjects of investigation are often difficult and sometimes impossible to observe, greater dependence traditionally has been placed on hypothesis formulation. The physical sciences are replete with examples of hypotheses that were substantiated by observation only after many decades, as improved experimental equipment became available.

Let us see if we can develop a very general picture of how observation and hypothesis formulation are integrated in the scientific methods. To begin with, we almost always find ourselves studying groups of objects or events that others have studied before us. We have, then, a backlog of observations and hypotheses about the group. Probably the reason for our study is that we are dissatisfied for one reason or another with previous hypotheses.

When existing hypotheses are inadequate, the researcher's task is to see whether he can suggest a new hypothesis that better explains prior observation, or one that is more logical. He attempts to revisualize the process or relationship. If his new hypothesis does not disagree with what is already known, if it is logically consistent internally, and if it appears to provide a better explanation of what is known, the researcher is ready to undertake additional observation.

The new hypothesis guides his observation. It tells him what to observe and how to relate his observations. New variables may be involved, or new relationships. Now further observation has a specific purpose—to test the power of his hypothesis. Does the hypothesis yield results that agree with actual fact as evidenced by observation?

Thus, observation and hypothesis formulation are interrelated. A body of observational fact helps us formulate new and perhaps better hypotheses, and these hypotheses guide our further observations.

Science is cumulative. Every study—each cycle—provides more information, deeper insight, and better generalizations about some segment of nature.

SOME ELEMENTAL CONCEPTS ABOUT SCIENTIFIC METHOD

Science is useful because it provides statements called laws or predictors. These allow us to foresee more or less correctly the outcome of natural events without waiting for the events to occur, and to estimate some attribute of nature without directly observing it. This is possible because nature is not entirely random; it contains strong elements of regularity and continuity. Each object or event is not really unique; it is similar to others, so experience relating to one item provides foreknowledge of others.

Scientific study has been remarkably adept at uncovering an underlying order and regularity to events that on the surface seem distinct and unrelated. This has lead many scientists to believe in a deterministic nature—a natural world totally governed by exact and unalterable relations or laws. In the determinist's view, if only we could describe objects and events completely enough, we would discover an absolute regularity and consistency admitting of no randomness or uncertainty. Even if nature were deterministic, no scientist would be likely to succeed completely in exorcising inconsistency. Our explanations seem always to be incomplete.

The existence of at least some degree of regularity, however, makes inductive reasoning useful. *Inductive reasoning* attributes to an entire class of objects or events those characteristics that have been regularly observed among a small number or sample of individuals from the class. The wedding of the concepts of mathematical probability with inductive logic—a truly fundamental advance in learning methods—has provided us with the ability to make more or less precise statements about the quality of experimental inductions; that is, about the probability of having arrived at an erroneous conclusion through inductive reasoning.

Deductive reasoning also has its place in the scientific method. Mathematics and formal logic provide formulas that allow one to proceed from an accepted premise to a conclusion that necessarily must follow. One of the simplest and oldest of these formulas is the syllogism, wherein a major premise (all men are mortal) is followed by a minor premise (Socrates is a man) from which can be deduced a conclusion (Socrates is mortal). All mathematical systems, however, have this same property of allowing a line of reasoning that is entirely internal once the premises are established. And mathematical reasoning can lead to useful conclusions that were not obvious from inspection of the premises. For example, through deductive logic the engineer can establish a satisfactory design for a bridge once certain basic premises, such as span, load, and materials, are established.

Causation has been a troubling concept to scientists. We often speak of natural processes as if there were some element of cause and effect inherent in them. Thus we say that changes in available moisture cause changes in tree growth; or that natural changes in stand composition are caused by differences in relative tolerance among tree species. What we have observed, however, is either association alone, or association and sequence.

Association of attributes or characteristics is simply the observation on repeated individuals that one characteristic always is associated with a second. For example, we can recognize tree species on the basis of gross characteristics such as bark texture and leaf form, but each species also has unique reproductive structures and wood anatomy. Thus a particular pattern of gross characteristics is always associated with a particular form of flower and fruit and a particular cellular structure. We do not assume that one of these characteristics caused the others; they simply always are found in association—all attributes of the organic unity and differentiation of the species.

In other circumstances we may observe sequence as well as association. For example, we may observe that seedlings invariably die after water is withheld. Lack of water causes the seedlings to die in the sense that death invariably follows the act of withholding water. Thus, cause implies both a necessary association and a sequence.

THE ROLE OF MODELS IN RESEARCH

The relationships of nature are so complex that researchers do not attempt to describe them completely. We deal instead with simplified abstractions called models (Skilling 1964).

A model is any simplified representation of an object, a relationship, or a system. Its intended use will determine which characteristics of reality the model should portray—only relevant information is presented. The simple nature of models enables us to use them to accumulate and to relate knowledge about reality which the complexity of reality tends to hide. An hypothesis is an example of a simple model; but a model may be sufficiently complex that a number of hypotheses can be extracted from it. Indeed, this manuscript describes a general model for research program planning; it also contains a model for project planning and another for study planning. And like all models, these too are simplifications of reality—useful simplifications, we hope.

Models are so fundamental to science that many treatises have been written about them. The use of models in biological (Thrall *et al.* 1967), economic (Ehrenberg 1966), behavioral (Dubin 1969), and other types of research are illustrated in references cited.

MODELS OF RELATIONSHIPS—AN EXAMPLE

A hypothetical example may help explain how models are used both in study planning and in interpreting observations. Undoubtedly, some early timber merchant observed that the volume of lumber cut from various trees was related to tree size. Perhaps he thought how useful it would be if he were able to predict—before a tree was felled—approximately what volume of lumber would be sawn from it. Subsequently, he might have reasoned that if he would measure the average volume of lumber that was being cut from 15-inch, 20-inch, and 25-inch trees..., then he could predict that similar amounts of lumber would be cut in the future from other trees with diameters of 15 inches, 20 inches, etc. So he observed logging and milling practices and developed a table of average lumber volumes for each tree-diameter class.

Perhaps it was a forester who observed later that on the better sites, the predicted lumber yields were consistently too low. The taller trees on these sites gave greater than average volumes. So he observed tree heights as well as diameters and developed a 2-way table relating average lumber yields for trees in each height class in each diameter class.

And finally a biometrician might have appeared. He was lazy—but smart. He reasoned that closer predictions could be made for individual trees if the data were summarized by 1-inch diameter classes and 1-foot height classes. He also reasoned that a tree was shaped something like a cone and thus that the relation between tree volume (V) and tree height (h) and diameter (dbh) was likely to be in the form $V = (1/3)$ (basal area) (height) $= (1/3) (\pi) (dbh)^2 (h)/2 = k(dbh)^2 (h)$. But for predicting lumber volumes in board feet, he thought that the available data on tree and lumber yield could be used to provide a more accurate constant, k, than $(1/3)\pi /2$. So he used the data on yields and tree sizes to estimate the constant k and thus derive a volume equation in the model form $V = k(dbh)^2 (h)$.

Note that each of these three used a model. In turn, each model was somewhat more complex than its predecessor. How did the models differ? The second model used two independent variables rather than one to indicate tree size. The third model differed from the second in the units used to measure tree size, in the form of the relationship postulated, and in the manner in which the relationship was described and computed.

Each model was a simplification—none described perfectly the relationship of tree size to lumber yield. Possibly many trees would have had to be cut before even one would have been found in which lumber yield was exactly predicted—yet even the imperfect predictions were useful. And complex models usually will give somewhat closer individual predictions than simple models.

The models were developed by first having a use in mind. The use identified the dependent factor, volume, and the appropriate units in which to measure it, board-feet of lumber sawed. Intended use also suggested that the independent factors should be easily estimated or measured variables that are related to volume in a more or less consistent and predictable manner—thus, first dbh, then dbh and height, and then a mathematical relationship $k(dbh)^2 (h)$.

MODEL CONSTRUCTION

Models can be developed from intensive formal knowledge of the relationships involved, from pure logic and, sometimes, from related disciplines. In the previous example, the third model came from simple solid geometry. As another example, models for evaluating the mechanical properties of wood have been obtained from the mathematics of electrical circuits. Most young researchers rely on a review of the research literature to suggest appropriate models. Unfortunately, too few put their personal knowledge, logic, and initiative to work in developing better ones.

If the researcher doesn't know what might constitute a reasonable model, quantification of relationships must be postponed until preliminary model building and testing have been completed. Model building is a very common form of research, quite appropriate in the problem-oriented context. The clientele for model-building research is almost always other researchers—or perhaps the model-building researcher himself.

Emphasis in model-building is on hypothesis formulation and testing, rather than on quantification of relationships. In fact, most studies that emphasize hypothesis testing have only model-building as an objective. Studies that are designed to build and test models are often the first step in a two-step process that has as its ultimate objective the quantification of a relationship. For example, the problem analysis may indicate a need for information about differences between the effects of two overstory conditions on deer browse. Unless past research has already indicated that actually there is a difference in browse under two forest conditions, the most efficient procedure for the first study may be to construct a model to test the hypothesis that no difference exists. The results of such a test, reviewed in light of the problem analysis, will indicate whether any differences that are discovered need to be reestimated, with greater precision, by a second study. The first study also provides information about the population in question, and thus permits a more efficient design of the follow-up study to qualify the differences more precisely. Models are also an essential prerequisite to developmental research, because simplified abstractions more readily lend themselves to creativity, and because models can be used to simulate a process before instituting it.

MODEL EVALUATION

Because a model is derived from observations of "real" experiences, it can be evaluated only in terms of how well it predicts other "real" experiences in similar situations. If a model is found to be inadequate for certain situations, then it is modified to better describe these situations. But the new model must itself then be tested against a new set of data to find out how well it predicts.

And so the cycle continues—deduction, observation, induction, model construction, observation, and model testing, induction and model improvement, etc. When do we stop? We stop when the model allows prediction within the accuracy and precision required for the intended use. A model can always be a little better, a little more exact—but always at a higher cost. And whether this cost is justified can only be determined by how the relationship is to be used.

The cost of selecting the wrong alternative differs from problem to problem; hence, the levels of precision and accuracy required of models used in the studies must differ. The user must recognize that a probability of error accompanies each use of a model. We have so much faith in some models that we even refer to them as laws. In others we have little confidence. But most of them are fallible if used outside the limits for which they were designed. "The validation of a model is not that it is 'true' but that it generates good testable hypotheses relevant to important problems" (Levins 1966).

KINDS OF MODELS

Models have been classified according to their physical form as iconic, analog, or symbolic. An iconic model is a physical replica of an object, usually on a different scale. Scale models of recreational areas are iconic models; so are models of wood fibers. Analog models also are physical representations of the real world, but the representation has been transposed to an unlike form. Maps, aerial photographs, and diagrams are analog models. Symbolic models represent reality by words, numbers, and other notation. Scientists find this class of models the most important because they are readily manipulated to deduce new concepts. Symbolic models may employ nominal, ordinal, or cardinal measurement processes.

Models may be either deterministic or probabilistic. When first formulated, models often are thought of as deterministic—an attempt is made to develop a complete description of the process. Because it is difficult or impractical, however, to include all determining variables and to hypothesize the exact relationship among them, models are seldom perfect. We recognize their imperfection or incompleteness by including in the model an error term that represents the discrepancy between predicted and observed results. Such a probabilistic interpretation is needed whenever we wish to establish the reliability of a model for prediction.

Models sometimes are classed as dynamic, recursive, sequential, or equilibrium models. These terms are used in somewhat different senses, but they all imply models that portray an adjustment process—that are capable of representing the response of the dependent factor to changes in the independent factors and of subsequent feedback and interaction.

Models may also be classed as prediction, maximization, or decision models. Prediction models provide an estimate of the value of the dependent variable, given values for the independent variable. Some models provide estimates of the maximum or minimum value of the dependent variable available within the permissible range of independent variable values. Statistical procedures are designed to select parameter estimates that minimize error, for example. Note that a maximization model contains, or is based on, a predictive relationship. So too with decision models. Decision models use discriminant functions or decision rules to select a course of action based on the value of the dependent variable that is estimated from independent variables. The statistical testing of hypotheses is based on such a model. The prediction error associated with a particular aspect of the model is identified (estimation) and is compared with the level of error that could be anticipated if the model component did not represent a "real" effect (decision rule).

The varieties of models that scientists may find to be useful representations of life are unlimited. There is no need to limit the models you use to those that fit existing hypotheses forms.

REFERENCES

BIOSCIENCE. 1966. Logic in biological investigation. (A series of papers by various authors.) BioScience 16(1):15-39.

DUBIN, R. 1969. Theory building. Free Press, New York. 298 p.

EHRENBERG, A. S. C. 1966. Laws in marketing: a tail-piece. Appl. Stat. 15(3):257-267.

FOREST, H. S., and H. GREENSTEIN. 1966. Biologists as philosophers. BioScience 16(11):783-788.

HESSE, M. B. 1966. Models and analogies in science. Univ. of Notre Dame Press, Notre Dame, Ind. 184 p.

LEVINS, R. 1966. The strategy of model building in population biology. Am. Scientist 54(4):421-431.

SKILLING, H. 1964. An operational view. Am. Scientist 52(4):388A-396A.

THRALL, R. M., J. A. MORTIMER, K. R. REBMAN, R. F. BAREM, ed. 1967. Some mathematical models in biology. Rev. ed. Report sponsored by University of Michigan, National Institutes of Health and Committee on Undergraduate Program in Mathematics.

5
DEFINING THE STUDY OBJECTIVE

A clear and reasonably specific study objective must be established before considering study procedures, but even the study objective is defined in a step-by-step fashion. You begin with a preliminary statement and gradually refine it until the final statement of objective is derived.

If a problem analysis has been made and a project plan prepared, you have a fine start. You will have specified the facts or relationships that are to be quantified, or the models, processes, or products that are to be developed. And you will have a reasonably clear understanding of how this information and the results of related studies are expected to be used in solving the specified problem. And even if a problem analysis and project plan have not been prepared, or if the objective of the research is to help define a problem, some similar thought process is needed to identify the study objective specifically and to consider how the information is most likely to be used in subsequent dependent research or, eventually, by managers.

A clearly defined objective for every research study is absolutely essential. Without a clear objective, you will have no valid basis for choosing appropriate study methods or materials for investigation, for knowing when the research is completed, for obtaining advice and support in conducting the study, for knowing what literature to review, or even for knowing where to begin.

Each study should have a single objective. Although it is efficient sometimes to seek two objectives simultaneously, it is usually better to think of this as two studies rather than one study with multiple objectives. If you do not limit your study to a single objective, you may collect data that are poorly suited for any single use and from which few valid inferences can be drawn. Useful research is more likely to arise from a well-aimed effort at a single, clearly defined target than from a scattergun attack at multiple and diffuse targets.

Clearly, study objectives precede the establishing of study procedures and provide the basis for selecting them. In defining the study objectives, however, it is important to consider what can and cannot be accomplished by research procedures. Almost invariably, the first statement of the study objective will not be the final statement. In planning a study, if the researcher finds he cannot achieve the study objective as originally specified, then he modifies his objective. Thus the two are interdependent, but the proper sequence is: first objective, then procedures.

To develop a study objective you need to make decisions of two kinds: how you intend to have your study results used and what specific data will be needed for these uses.

INTENDED USE OF STUDY RESULTS

Formally or informally, implicitly or explicitly, every study planner as a first step in study planning answers several questions about the intended use of his study results . Of course it is possible to conduct studies before explicitly considering how the results will be used. The use questions, however, will actually have been answered implicitly by the objectives and procedures that have been selected. Logically then, you should raise and consciously answer these use questions when you are establishing the study objectives. You can derive the answers just as clearly at this time. And in addition your study procedures can still be formulated to provide the kind of information that would indeed be most useful.

The four basic use questions are: Should the results be qualitative or quantitative? Is a particular measure of validity required? Will data be used for analysis or for simple prediction? What is the population to which the results are to be applied?

Qualitative vs. Quantitative Results

The researcher intends all study results to be descriptive, but the description may be either in words or numbers. Qualitative descriptions are common when the objective of the research is problem analysis. The biologist who describes the life cycle of a plant or animal is defining in part the context of those choice problems that have to do with manipulation of that plant or animal. Much public policy research focuses on definition of a problem's context. But the objective of your research may also be to define more specifically a decision-maker's objective or those alternatives available to him. In fact, the process of problem definition is for the most part qualitative. Qualitative descriptions are prerequisite to quantitative ones, and usually they are less expensive.

But qualitative descriptions are not very exact; frequently words mean different things to different people. And it is difficult to apply inductive logic to them. For these reasons most research, both basic and applied, proposes to obtain quantitative results—numerical estimates of either specific parameters or relationships between them. Some studies intentionally produce both qualitative and quantitative results. If your objective is to develop a process for measuring air pollution, the results will likely consist of a qualitative description of the process and a quantitative description of its effectiveness. Or, if your objective is to develop a model describing how wood shrinks, the results could be qualitative, quantitative, or both, depending on their intended use.

Measure of Validity; Precision Required

If you are seeking a numerical estimate of a fact or relationship you must decide whether your clientele will need an objective measure of the validity of your estimate. If so, just how precise must your estimate be? For example, if they need a measure of validity you will have to specify a maximum acceptable standard error; you should know how small a change or difference the users will want to detect, at a specified probability level. Measures of validity require costlier forms of research: for example, several samples are needed rather than one and of course, precise estimates cost more than rough estimates.

Simple Prediction vs. Analysis or Control

If your objective involves estimating a relationship, you must decide whether this relationship will be used for prediction only, or for analysis and control. Simple prediction implies that the relationship will be used to estimate values of the dependent variable from measured values of the independent variables on individuals from essentially the same population sampled in the study. For example, relationships developed to predict how intensively outdoor recreation facilities will be used are of this nature. These relationships are intended to estimate the most likely level of recreational use after measuring the size of the area, the distance to population centers, anticipated weather conditions, and other factors.

But the intended use of other relationships may be analysis or control rather than simple prediction. For example, you (or perhaps more precisely, your clientele) may wish to make explanatory cause-effect inferences from the relationship you will derive from your research. Or you may want a relationship you can use to estimate the response in the dependent variable if the independent variables are manipulated by applying resource management practices, for example. These uses are analytical and interpretative. They involve inferences about structural or functional relations in the natural population. The prediction of change implies an assumption of functional relations, cause and effect. These are the kinds of relationships needed if one wishes to affect the dependent variable by controlling the independent variables. Relationships suitable for such analytical or control purposes often are more difficult to derive than those to be used only for predicting single values of the dependent variable.

An additional example might further clarify the differences between simple prediction and analysis. You and your clientele might use simple prediction to estimate the growth of individual stands from observations of the slope, soil texture, and available nitrogen. But the use would be analytical if you wanted to be able to say something about the *independent* effect of nitrogen on growth, about the physiological mechanism by which nitrogen affects growth, or about the effect on growth of adding more nitrogen. Research to accomplish the simple-prediction goals would be relatively easy to accomplish by field observations, but the analytical uses would require much more controlled, sophisticated, and expensive study procedures.

Applicable Population
        And in all studies, you must know the population to which your results will be applied. Scope is the word sometimes loosely used in this context. For example, if you intend to develop a relationship between tree-surface indicators of heart-rotting fungi and the amount of heart rot in Douglas-fir trees, you must know whether your clientele will want to use this relationship primarily in Oregon's Lane County, in the Willamette watershed, in the Northwest, or throughout the entire range of Douglas-fir. In each case, a somewhat different study would be appropriate; the population you would sample would be determined by the target population.

Some studies are conducted to provide information that is extremely well tailored for solving one specific problem, but are inappropriate for solving others. Other studies take the other approach, providing data that are fairly well suited for solving several similar problems but are not ideally suited for any one. An example is the prediction of water yield from snowpack—should the researcher construct a relationship for each watershed? or each state? or each region? Obviously, the solution depends on the anticipated users. How important is an accurate estimate to each group? How "differentiated" are the areas a specific user will be sampling?

Deciding on the most efficient approach is never a simple matter. But before the researcher decides to obtain the best possible data for solving the very specific problem of one client, he should consider whether his study objective might be broadened to provide data that would help directly in solving other problems that have similar information needs.

Generally, the population that we must deal with is not unique. We can define the population broadly or narrowly in almost any study. Several factors guide us, however. First, we know that in general the broader the population the more complex the process that yields the desired result. For example, we would probably have to consider many more factors to explain differences in site quality over half a dozen states than in only one county. Therefore we often choose to deal with restricted populations so that we can keep our models simple.

On the other hand, by dealing with broad populations we can introduce more generality. That is, our models contain more information because they apply to more individuals. And we can unify our concepts by describing with a single relationship outcomes that previously may have been thought of as essentially different. What we are willing to attempt in scope of population often is limited by the extent of past study. Usually we are successful with studies involving broad populations only after good hypotheses have been formulated and tested for individual segments.

Use-Objective Relationships—an Example

How use considerations influence the selection of study objectives and procedures can be illustrated by another example.

Let's assume that information about the growth of uneven-aged northern hardwood stands is required as a part of a larger project to develop management guides for this timber type. A survey of available information has revealed serious limitations and a new study has been requested. Do we now have all the information we will need to design the study? Let's dig a little deeper.

"Growth" seems like a fairly adequate description of the attribute of interest, but it really is not. First, we will need to know how many different growth estimates are needed. Are the overall objectives of the research project (*i.e.*, the ultimate needs of the clientele) such that a single estimate of average growth for the entire timber type would be sufficient? Or are separate growth estimates needed for various site and stand conditions, and for different programs of management?

Second, we will need to be much more precise about what we mean by "growth." What is it that we actually should measure? Is it total cubic-foot growth, is it board-foot merchantable growth, or is it the growth of merchantable portions of merchantable trees, gross or net, total or by species and log grade? Once again the attribute can be defined adequately only in terms of the use the data will be put to. What kind of "growth" do the users need information about?

What is our population? Well, we've said it above: uneven-aged hardwood stands. Not quite. We must be much more specific. What do we mean by uneven-aged? Are we talking only about stands that contain trees of widely different ages, or do we include any stand that departs from a strictly even-aged condition? How do we define a hardwood stand? Do we exclude any stand containing conifers, or do we allow our population to include stands, say, with up to 10 percent coniferous volume? Our first job in defining a population, then, is to strive for clarity and objectivity, so that there can be no question about what we include and what we exclude.

We also have to make sure that everything we include in our population is really available for observation. Suppose we intend to study the recreational use of private campgrounds in the New England states, but because of travel restrictions we can take field observations only within one hundred miles of Laconia, New Hampshire. We had better recognize this restriction in our definition of the population, and in deciding whether the study is really worth undertaking if we must live with such a restriction. Nonavailability can be much more subtle than this, of course. For instance we often unconsciously avoid observation in difficult-to-reach locations, or of difficult-to-handle materials.

We must remember too that the definition of a population specifies the users of the resulting information. And once again, it is only by knowing who will use this information that we can select an appropriate population.

The precision of information should be related to the cost of being wrong. Precision refers to the likelihood or probability of our estimates of campground use being within a stated deviation from the true value. For example, we may choose to provide growth estimates that have a 90 percent probability of being within 10 percent of the true values of growth. Notice, it is at this point in our planning that we first recognize that we cannot provide perfectly precise information.

The more precise we choose to be, the greater the research effort, time, and cost required. And we want to be sure that any added efforts to achieve greater precision result in a commensurate benefit to the user. So again we must consider the user. How critical is this item of information? How accurate must it be to prevent serious error? Sometimes crude information will suffice. For example, a tree breeder, attempting to develop for Christmas tree growers a Scotch pine hybrid with improved color, may decide that a modest improvement would be without practical significance. In this situation a rather crude estimate of improvement is all that is required.

DEFINING THE INFORMATION OF INTEREST

A study objective must define precisely the information of interest. How can you design a questionnaire for survey research if you have not clearly specified what you wish to find out? The same is true for case studies. And if you are developing a new product, you can make little progress until you have an adequate set of specifications. Most resources research involves relationships, their formulation, testing, or quantification. If your study objective involves either testing an hypothesis about a relationship or direct quantification of a relationship, you must first describe the relationship.

Three steps are used in describing the information of interest. The first is identifying the key factors involved, such as volume, height, and diameter in the common volume-table relationship. Next, you choose variables to measure or represent these factors. For example, for the factor volume you might choose the variable gross bole volume in cubic feet, from a 1.5-foot stump to an 8-inch top; for height, height in tenths of a foot from ground level to stem tip; and so forth. Finally, for relationships you describe the form or nature of the relationship between the dependent and the independent variables, whether it is linear, of the form V = (a) (dbh^2) (Ht), or some other. Let's examine each of these three steps in more detail.

Key Factors

The first step is to specify the key factors or characteristics to be observed. For the anatomist, this may mean listing the types of cell wall layers to be measured. Or for the model builder these key factors are the types of elements that make up the model. For instance, a model of a seedling's growth might include such factors as intensity of sunlight, water supply, and nutrient supply. If your objective is to quantify a relationship, you must identify the dependent and independent factors.

The dependent factor is that characteristic of the item of interest that we wish to predict. For example, if we were interested in coho salmon, and more particularly in knowing the numbers of coho salmon fry we could expect in a given stream, we would first have to know something about the fecundity of the female salmon. Here, fecundity would be the dependent factor to be predicted in an early study, and the salmon fry population the dependent factor to be predicted by a later study.

Independent factors are those general characteristics that differ with variations in the dependent factor, and which are easy to observe or measure. They may be looked upon as the general sources of variation in the system. If, for another example, the dependent factor were tree volume, the independent factors might be tree dimensions such as height, diameter, and form. Or if the dependent factor were stand growth, the independent factors could include site quality, stand density, and species. Usually there will be a long list of independent factors. Identifying all likely independent factors requires the researcher to use his detailed knowledge of forestry, biology, economics, and other fields, and may make use of both observation and analogy.

Selecting Variables to Measure the Factors

Seldom is it possible to measure a "factor" directly. We thus use "variables" as quantifiable and specific descriptions of the "factors." The term factor refers to those general characteristics that the researcher wishes to estimate or evaluate. In contrast, the term variable is used to refer to a very specific measure or index that is selected to represent or describe the factor. For example, foresters often use the variable, site index, as an indirect measure of the more general factor, site quality, and dbh as a measure of tree size.

Sometimes any of several variables may be used, or a combination of them. Again, if site quality is the factor, then variables such as aspect in degrees of azimuth, slope in percent, and soil texture may, when taken together, provide a reasonably good index. In some cases, the variable may simply be a much-refined definition of the (more general) factor. We are more inclined to think in terms of factors but to conduct research we must refine our thinking to measurable identities, namely, variables.

The final statement of study objectives (and the resulting parameters or relationships) must always be expressed in terms of specific variables. And because the parameters in a relationship depend so much on which variables are selected, the results may provide only a general indication of the relationship between the factors. This point should be remembered when evaluating the study results in terms of factor relationships.

Thus the next step is to choose the variables that will be used to measure the selected factors. But no general rule can identify the best variable to use. A precise description is needed for each variable. This includes a definition of the unit or element that will be considered as providing an observation. It also includes specifying the measurement precision and scale of measurement.

For example, in studies of heat exchange in forest communities, a dependent variable is needed for the factor, heat. A suitable variable might be "incoming solar radiation measured above the canopy in gram-calories per square centimeter per minute, to the nearest 0.01 g.c." Or, in some cases, temperature or net radiation might be better than solar radiation as a variable to measure "heat." The measurement precision used for the independent variables should of course be related to the precision desired in the estimate of the dependent variable; care may be required to keep the two in balance.

The Study Hypothesis

When the study is designed to quantify a relationship, the study hypothesis is specified by describing the mathematical nature of the relationship among the variables. This relationship should be evident, to some degree, from the model obtained earlier. The research planner may at this stage specify only whether the relationship is linear, whether it is expected to be positive or negative, and whether there are interacting relationships, *i.e.*, whether some of the independent variables are interacting in their relationship with the dependent factor. The relationship can then be checked for logical form and internal consistency simply by applying the rules of logic.

SUMMARY

It is impossible to overemphasize the importance of completely specifying your study objective. This is true even though you realize you are likely to modify this initial statement before your study planning is completed.

When the study objective involves a relationship, the dependent and independent factors must be identified. Appropriate variables must be selected to represent these factors. And the form of the relationship among the variables must be specified.

Fully specifying the study objective requires an indication of how the study results will be used and the population to which they will be applied. You must determine whether your results are to be used for simple prediction or analysis. You must decide whether a measure of the validity of your results is required, and if so, what precision will be adequate.

Is all this really necessary? We believe so. We have found that it is in the process of defining study objectives that most young researchers go astray. At best, poorly defined objectives mean a lot of time wasted later in back tracking; at worst, poor objectives may make it impossible to complete the research, or to use the results.

REFERENCES

KEMPTHORNE, O. 1952. Design and analysis of experiments. Wiley, N.Y. 631 p.

PLATT, J. R. 1964. Strong inference. Science 146:347-353.

WILM, H. G. 1952. A pattern of scientific inquiry for applied research. J. Forestry 50:120-125.

6

SELECTING
STUDY PROCEDURES

In the previous chapter we stressed the importance of a well-defined study objective, and discussed specifically how to define one. We related the study objective back to the problem analysis and, at the same time, we anticipated the study procedures.

This order—first objective, then procedures—is important because it is the objective that determines the procedures. It is not logical to pick a study procedure and then take as the study objective the job that procedure can do. At best, this approach leads to the "right answer to the wrong question."

On what basis does the researcher choose among the many study procedures that he might use? As a first criterion, he considers only those procedures that will satisfy his study objective. The second criterion is efficiency. The researcher chooses the procedure that satisfies the objective with least effort, materials, and time. This is not easy because many complex things influence efficiency. Nevertheless, it is important. Scientists are developing new research techniques to expand the number of study objectives for which we have logical procedures, and to provide more efficient procedures for achieving a given objective.

When procedures are not readily available for achieving the most desirable study objective, however, one cautiously uses feedback to revise the study objective to accommodate what is possible. Study planning thus proceeds through successive stages and revisions, continually referring to the problem analysis to assure that the final plan will lead to a study that does indeed solve the intended problem.

The main criterion for selecting procedures is that they satisfy the study objective efficiently. An efficient procedure must take into account the entire context of the study, *i.e.*, the nature of the fact or relationship defined in the study objective, and the nature of the population to which the results are to apply.

Because natural resources research involves scientists of many disciplines, an almost infinite number of specific study procedures have been developed. Many variations of "case study" or "survey" procedures have been developed for qualitative research. Simulation procedures, particularly valuable for developmental research, are as varied as the developments they have helped produce. Experimental procedures are even more numerous.

Every problem, every needed relationship, and every resulting study objective could lead to a different procedure. Hence we will not deal with the specific methods of research. Instead we shall focus on the more general aspects of selecting study procedures—those aspects that transcend the details of making observations. These broad procedural questions must be considered in study planning *before* the researcher proceeds to the details of methods. Those who conduct research are expected to be familiar with both the philosophical and the practical aspects of scientific methods and with the relationship between general scientific methods and particular study procedures. Among the many good books on these subjects are those by Whitehead (1925), Conant (1951), Kempthorne (1952), Wilson (1952), Bross (1953), Cohen (1944), and Ackoff (1962).

STATISTICS AND RESOURCES RESEARCH

Statistical methods are an important group of study procedures by which many study objectives can be achieved most efficiently. Every researcher is expected to understand and be proficient in those statistical methods relevant to research in his subject matter specialty. Wilson (1952, p. 169) said, for example,

"The science of statistics has been developed for the purpose of assisting in the separation of chance effects from true regularities. An understanding of its basic principles is essential for all scientists, regardless of the rigor and precision of their disciplines."

However, even those well informed about statistical methods often miss the link between study objectives and study procedures. The link remains missing because particular statistical methods are emphasized by statistical references but particular data needs are emphasized by the researcher.

For example, the elegant experimental design cited in the textbook often does not really satisfy the study objective that arose from the problem analysis. Does this mean that statistical methods are irrelevant? Certainly not. It simply means that the statistical method must be designed and selected to be relevant for the specific study objective. Statistical methods are only the *means* of achieving the study objective, not an *end* in themselves.

The Researcher and the Statistical Consultant

After the data have been collected, researchers are often tempted to seek assistance in "finding out what's in this batch of data." Usually statistical methods cannot help much with such questions. Statistical data analysis at the end of the study will prove useful *only* if the groundwork for its use has been laid in the planning and conduct of the preceding research.

The idealized experimental methods of science have been described earlier as a pattern of:
(1) deductive reasoning and model construction
(2) designing experiment
(3) collecting data
(4) checking data for concordance with a *prior* model
(5) inductive inference to population
(6) revision of model, and
(7) back around the circle again until the model is sufficiently precise for the applications intended

Where are statistical methods useful in this endeavor? Commonly they are used as steps (4) and (5), but the validity of their use depends on appropriately planning steps (1), (2), and (3).

Notice that the model is determined from prior considerations; that the experimental design follows from the model and context of the experiment; and that we make a statistical test about whether the data are convincingly out of concordance with the model, that is, whether differences are more than expected by chance. This test is possible only if the model is constructed before the experiment. Certainly you would expect data to be in concordance with a model that is indeed derived from those very data! In this latter case we have succeeded only in describing the data; we have no basis for testing the model's ability to describe the population that gave rise to the data.

When consulted at the last analytical stage by a researcher with collected data in hand, the statistical consultant must assume that the researcher has made all the appropriate prior plans. The statistician could have advised the researcher earlier about procedures for model building. But now, because the consultant is not an expert in the subject matter that gave rise to the model and the data, he naturally assumes that all this has been done by the researcher before the experimental plan was developed. On the other hand, the researcher often wrongly thinks of these preliminaries merely as details of statistical method and assumes that they are the responsibility of the statistical consultant. These combined attitudes result in misunderstanding and the omission of important research planning. This can lead to patching together questionable inferences from expensive data. Close teamwork and understanding between researcher and statistician are required before the data are collected, and many hours of discussion usually are needed for complex studies.

The Pursuit of Significance

Another common consequence of the "missing link" is overemphasis on achieving a result that can be called statistically significant. It is easy to fall into the habit of seeking some way, after the data are collected, to have the test of significance yield "positive results." Though not obvious to the neophyte researcher, this is a serious violation of the intent of scientific methods and of statistical methods in particular. Fortunately, we are less often affected by this malady when we emphasize estimating parameters rather than testing hypotheses.

One consequence of this "pursuit of significance" is that the researcher may delude himself about the results of his study. He may decide that the differences in his data indicate both real and important differences in the population, when they do not.

Every scientist understands, when he reflects on it, that real differences among study data need not imply analogous "real" differences (in the probability sense) in the population sampled. And every scientist understands that "statistically significant" is not at all synonomous with "operationally important." But in the relentless pursuit of significance we tend to forget this, so the beginning researcher may find it helpful to think carefully about what the hypothesis test means.

In the real world around us, any two things or groups of things differ in some characteristic. At any given time, we may not find this difference to be important in the conduct of our affairs or in our current understanding of the world around us. At another time and in other circumstances, however, we might wish to exploit the difference. Then the difference becomes important. If we adopt the proposition that all things differ, then we may generally view our research as being concerned with finding out how big the differences are, and what causes the differences.

Now, consider any two groups of trees that are believed to differ in average diameter. The question is: How much, and is it important? We must agree that if we measure all the trees we could decide how big the difference between average diameters is, accept it as real and decide whether it is important. To this point, statistical methods cannot help us except perhaps to control measurement error in making the observations. But if we wish to observe only a small sample of trees from each group to decide how big the difference is, then statistics can help us. But a statistical test of hypothesis does not tell us how large the difference is. If we know how large a difference is important, a statistical test of hypothesis will tell us the probability that this large a difference between sample means would arise by chance *if there were no real difference* between the average diameters of the two groups. The test gives only a *relative* measure of how large the difference between averages of the two groups appears to be—based on the relative differences in variation among individuals in a group vs. between groups sampled. We have acknowledged the difference in individual tree diameters to be greater than zero, so the test will not indicate whether the actual absolute difference between the groups is large enough to be distinguished from zero. But we can estimate an absolute difference with arbitrary precision by making the sample large enough. Similarly, we can detect arbitrarily small differences as being significant with a sufficiently large experiment. But whether a difference can be absolutely distinguished from zero is not a statistical question and it is not likely to be the objective of forest-resources research.

Headlong pursuit of significance leads us to design larger and larger, and more and more rigidly controlled experiments so that we may detect as statistically significant a smaller and smaller difference. This emphasis acknowledges no optimum level of time and money spent. If, on prior consideration, we specify the difference that it is important to detect at given probability levels, then we can determine the size of sample or experiment and the level of experimental error necessary to detect such a difference if it exists. If we ignore this specification we might find ourselves testing for infinitesimal and unimportant differences. And we could repeatedly test hypotheses of "no difference" when we already have overwhelming evidence that there is a difference large enough to be important—e.g., plant growth vs. nitrogen level in soil.

Sometimes researchers are disappointed with, and even suppress, study results that do not show "significant" differences. Such results are even sometimes called "negative results." This implies that we do not need to know that a difference is small. The decision-maker who will use the relationship provided by the study will certainly need to know if the response to a certain treatment is small.

Other dangers exist in discounting the evidence for studies that do not show "significance." We expect a certain percentage (determined by the "level of significance") of our experiments to indicate that a difference does actually exist, its measurement depending on the power of the test and the sensitivity of the experiment. So in accumulating evidence by combining results of several studies, we will be misled unless we also include the experiments that did not show "significance" (Bross 1953, chap. 5).

Hypothesis Testing vs. Quantification of Relationships

Many studies are designed to test an hypothesis about whether one variable changes significantly with changes in another variable. Actually, these studies are aimed at quantifying relationships—eventually. And of course one must estimate a relationship to test any hypothesis about it. But in such studies, the objective does not stress estimating the magnitude of the change in this particular phase of the research. This may be simply because the objective has been put into statistical terms with traditional stress on hypothesis testing.

But when study objectives arise from decision problems, an estimate of the change or difference is usually needed by the decision-maker to solve his problem—not simply knowledge that a significant difference exists. A man choosing among alternatives is not likely to find the following statement particularly helpful:

Differences as large as those observed in this experimental material would be expected by chance alone to occur no more than 5 times in 100 such experiments with material having a true average difference of zero and a true variance equal to the estimate obtained for random error in this experiment.

Yet, strictly speaking, this is what is said or implied directly from studies designed to test the ordinary null hypothesis. This is the statistical interpretation of an experiment with the conventional test of treatment effects indicated "significant" at 0.05 probability. Actually, of course, the real objective of such research is usually not just to test the hypothesis that there is no difference, but to quantify or estimate that difference. For, as Bacon held, the objective of all science is to quantify; he argued that what we cannot quantify we do not know.

Why, then, do we often choose merely to test an hypothesis, when this appears to be a case of quitting with the job only half done? The reason is that hypothesis-testing studies are relatively easy and inexpensive to conduct; estimation of a specific relationship, with sufficient precision to make the results useful, is more costly. Thus you will frequently conduct studies to test hypotheses before you design others to quantify the relationships. The former will indicate which differences or changes are worth further effort to quantify more precisely.

STUDY PROCEDURES AND STATISTICAL DESIGN

Statistical analysis helps the resources researcher to find out efficiently what his data mean—if the analysis is planned when the other study procedures are planned. The form of analysis is limited by the methods used to collect the data so statistical methods must be considered when variables are defined and their interrelationship are assumed, when sample material is selected, and when methods are selected to observe the variables.

Sources of Variation; Variables to Quantify Them

In developing the study objective, the researcher will have listed the independent factors (and then variables) related to the dependent factor. For example, some of the common sources of variation encountered in research about outdoor recreation preferences are income, occupation, education, and age. In selecting study procedures, the list of variables should be made as specific and all-inclusive as possible.

The researcher must decide how each source of variation will be handled in the study. First, he selects an appropriate variable to represent or quantify each factor. Then the researcher decides whether to handle that variable as:

(a) a treatment, the level of which will be manipulated and measured

(b) a covariate, not under the control of the experimenter, but to be measured to improve the estimate of relationship or the sensitivity of any tests of hypothesis about it, or to aid in interpretation by evaluating effects of extraneous or concomitant sources of variation

(c) a predictive variable, to be measured in the combinations and at the levels at which it occurs naturally without control

(d) an extraneous source of variation, the effect of which will be averaged out by randomization techniques in the sampling or experimental design

(e) an unimportant source of variation, and thus disregarded (except for its influence as a source of random variation in experimental error or sampling error)

The levels at which treatment variables will be controlled must be specified, and these justified by the study objective.

Many things are considered in choosing the most appropriate of several possible variables to use as measures of a selected factor. Most of these depend on the use specified in the study objective. For example, the precision in measuring the independent variables depends on the precision required in the estimates of the dependent variable. Frequently we may choose to give up some precision so that we can use a variable that is easier to measure.

From the use to be made of a relationship, the researcher may be able to determine whether it will be more desirable to define the variable in discrete classes (as attributes or classifying variables) rather than in a continuous form, or to search for a way of expressing in a continuous form what is customarily thought of as a qualitative variable such as species or aspect.

Some variables can be measured with consistency from one observer to the next, and when remeasurements are to be made this may be important in determining the best variable to use. For example, in estimating the board-foot volume of trees at one occasion, having merchantable height as an independent variable will give higher precision in the estimated volume. If, however, we want to estimate tree growth from the difference between the tree-volume estimates obtained at two different times, we cannot tolerate the rather large inconsistency between observations of merchantable height as it is usually defined. Thus we may want either to select a definition that can be more consistently applied or to give up the variable entirely.

If the desired relationship is intended for simple prediction, the researcher need only be concerned with specifying independent variables that can be measured and can be expected to be good predictors of the dependent variable. But if the relationship we are trying to estimate will be used for analytical purposes, then we must choose variables to closely represent the factors the user wishes controlled and that are thought to be linked directly with the changes in the dependent variable.

If the relationship will be used for predictive purposes only, then the researcher will select independent variables that are highly correlated with the dependent variable but as little correlated with each other as possible. Each such variable added as a predictor will increase the precision of estimate more than would a variable highly correlated with determining variables already used.

Relationship and Statistical Model

The independent variables will be interrelated; knowing this will help to hypothesize the relationship between the dependent and the various independent variables. The variables will need redefining to conform to the hypothesized relationship, then vice versa, and so on, until a reasonable form is reached. In our tree volume example we would probably begin with dbh (diameter breast high) as the first approximation of a variable, D, used as a measure of the factor, diameter. But when we consider the theory of solid geometry that provides our first approximation of the relationship, we realize that volume is proportional to the square of diameter for solids that have circular cross sections. We realize it is proportional to the product of total height, H, and the square of diameter, D, so we hypothesize the relationship for volume, V, as: $V = K(D^2 H)$, based on variables to be defined for the factors "diameter" and "height."

In further defining these variables we must keep in mind both the character of the model and the intended use of the relationship. For example, we realize that for geometric solids like cones, the diameter is that at the base. Our goal, however, is efficient prediction, and we know that the diameter of a tree at ground level varies irregularly in cross section, and is difficult to measure in practice. Hence, we select dbh and revise the model accordingly.

This connection between the definition of variables and the specification of a relationship is common. The result can be written as an equation that is specific in the form of relationship and form of each variable, so it should show whether the relationship is linear, exponential, or otherwise, and whether the variables in the equation are to be in arithmetic, exponential, logarithmic, or some other form.

We have now reconsidered the sources of variation and the variables selected to represent each source, we have decided how each source of variation will be handled, and we have refined both the descriptions of the variables and the form of the relationship between the dependent and independent variables. We are now ready to specify the statistical model and method appropriate to the study.

Method of Analysis

The objective of the study has pointed toward a primary estimate of a parameter or a relationship. The form of statistical analysis will be indicated by the objective of the study, the statistical nature of the population, the model chosen to represent the population, and the methods of controlling and measuring the variables.

The study planner will first describe, in statistical terms, the parameters or the relationships that are to be estimated or tested. This will include the complete specification of the statistical model. And if hypotheses are to be tested, they will be specified in the form of null hypotheses. The researcher must examine the study conditions to see whether they will meet the assumptions of the proposed statistical model and analysis. If these assumptions are to be tested during the execution of the study, this must be specified. If transformations are required to make the variables conform more closely to the statistical assumptions, these too must be described and justified.

If analysis of variance or covariance is involved, it will be helpful to set up the analysis-of-variance table with the sources of variation and degrees of freedom listed. If any unorthodox calculations are anticipated for estimating the mean-squares or obtaining test statistics, such calculations should be described.

The researcher must be specific about the requirements for objectively evaluating the validity of estimate or test, putting the requirements into numerical and statistical terms. For example, he must specify the acceptable level of significance or confidence and, for tests of hypotheses, how small a difference he wants to detect at the given level of significance. The level of significance depends upon the acceptable risk of rejecting a true null hypothesis (Type I error); the confidence level depends upon the confidence that we wish to place in an estimate. In some studies, particularly those having objectives that specify a low risk of accepting a false null hypothesis, we may want to make some statement about the Type II error. For example, Type II error would be especially important if you were screening materials for a cure for a major tree disease or a control for a major forest pest. You do not want to discard an effective material. The size of sample or experiment that is required can then be calculated from these specifications. The objectives and methods of analysis may also be modified to take advantage of the speed and efficiency of electronic data processing.

Selecting Sample Material

The researcher must carefully and specifically describe the method of selecting samples or experimental units, and the number of samples or units to be taken. The method of taking samples is determined largely by the study objective, the statistical model, and the proposed method of analysis. The characteristics and physical location of the population and the study material, however, sometimes impose limitations on the sampling or experimental design. Thus, these too must be considered in choosing the samples and the form of analysis.

When the study objective involves the statistical testing of an hypothesis, the test will require a statistical theory appropriate to the population, to the relationship between the variables in that population (the statistical model), to the method of selecting samples and experimental materials, and to the methods of randomization or other control in the experiment. The hypothesis also will have to be put into a "testable" form; we can't prove things right, we can only prove them wrong, usually as a null hypothesis.

If the hypothesis involves variables over which the researcher has no control, he can only sample combinations of the values of the various independent and dependent variables as they occur naturally in the population and use inductive inference to estimate or interpret the relationship. Here a test of hypothesis about relationship is according to the theory of regression analysis for nonexperimental data and the inference is necessarily weak (Kempthorne 1952; Blalock 1961; Platt 1964).

If all the independent variables are under the control of the researcher, then the tests of the usual hypotheses are straightforward and follow the experimental design used to control the variation. The inference is potentially stronger than when the researcher has no control (Kempthorne 1952). And when the level of significance, level of Type II error, and size of difference to be detected by the test are all specified, the number of samples, replicates, etc., can be calculated.

If, in estimating relationships, the reliability of estimates of the dependent variable does not need to be measured objectively, then we need take only enough sampling units to estimate the relationship from simultaneous equations or by graphical procedures. If a measure of validity is required, however, then in addition to having more sampling units than independent variables, the samples must be selected randomly with respect to the dependent variable and the parameters must be estimated by a statistical technique, the most common one being least-squares regression.

When the relationship is to be used for analytical purposes, the method of analysis and sampling procedures would not be too difficult if the independent variables were not related to each other. Then an appropriate multiple-regression equation could be fitted to the appropriate independent variables observed on a properly selected sample.

Unfortunately, in natural populations the independent variables are almost always intercorrelated. Under these conditions it is not possible to observe, by sampling uncontrolled variables in nature, what actually happens to the dependent variable when all but one of the independent variables are held constant, and this one is permitted to vary. If an independent variable co-varies with one or more of the other independent variables, then they will both be observed only in related combinations; any change observed in the dependent variable can only be interpreted as being associated with the joint occurrence of that combination of the independent variables. Put another way, we cannot observe independent effects of the many "causal" variables and we cannot assess the results of independent causes. The possible inferences are weak and generally the researcher, being aware of the pitfall of interpreting correlation as evidence of sequence, is left to make only statements about the association. If the independent variables are not controllable, then the researcher may have no alternative but to use nonexperimental study procedures. By sampling entirely at random he will at least be able to obtain estimates of the validity of such parameters of association as correlation coefficients.

If the independent variables can be controlled by the researcher either by adjusting their levels or by randomizing designs, then it is possible to make much "stronger" estimates of the changes in the dependent variables that can be expected from changes in individual independent variables. Cause-effect inferences are then possible because the researcher can, in his sample, observe the actual effect of manipulating single independent variables, and to the degree that extraneous variation has been controlled, the researcher may infer from his experiment that "this change in X causes or leads to this change in Y." For a more complete discussion of these points see introduction to Kempthorne (1952), *Design and Analysis of Experiments*, Blalock (1961), *Causal Inference in Nonexperimental Research* and Platt (1964), *Strong Inferences*.

If the validity of an estimate of change is to be measured, then the samples or experimental material must be selected randomly or with a known probability of occurrence from the population to which the estimates and inferences are to apply. And there must be samples enough to estimate the variation around the sample means. If the inferences or estimates are to apply only to those individuals included in the sample or experiment, or if no objective measure of validity is required, then sampling with unknown probability might be used. In this case, it would be necessary only to take the minimum number of samples required to estimate the relationship itself.

The appropriate number of samples (or size of experiment) is related to:

(1) the required precision, as specified under objectives
(2) the chosen level of significance or probability
(3) the variability in the population studied, and
(4) the cost of sampling.

Each sampling design or experimental design requires a different expression for calculating the number of samples required. Given such an expression, the researcher can use the chosen level of precision and available information on variances, ranges, and means to estimate roughly the required number of replications or samples. In sampling for estimating a parameter we must also decide how to allocate sampling units by strata, clusters, stages, and phases.

A rule must be specified as to how the plots, blocks, or other sampling and experimental units will be selected. For example, plots and blocks might be laid out as a randomized block, split-plot design; samples might be taken at random within strata. A diagram of field layout is helpful, if not actually necessary. The sizes of plots and widths of isolation strips must be chosen and their boundaries defined.

Methods of Observation, Data Collection, and Experimental Control
The method of observing the variables is important for statistical procedures. In study planning the researcher must think through the procedures to be used in
  (1) handling or treating experimental material, controlling treatments, etc.
  (2) setting up the study in field, laboratory, greenhouse, etc.
  (3) taking and recording measurements, observations, and photographs

Experimental apparatus must be designed and tested. Questionnaires must be developed. Measuring units and devices must be selected. Tally sheets must be prepared or automatic recording devices set up. The list of such important, costly, and time-consuming activities is nearly inexhaustible.

Each study objective will require a different set of these procedures. Some will require elaborate methods of observation and experimental control. Analysis of a given natural-resource problem may lead to study objectives involving facts and relationships from any branch of science or from several branches—biological, physical, and social. And each branch of science requires many different methods of observation and experimental control. These methods are treated in detail in the literature of each branch. For example, for biological science some of the major methods of apparatus design, chemical analysis, and measurement of wave length, are detailed by Van Norman (1963) and Newman (1965). For biological science directly concerned with the environment, methods are detailed by Andrewartha (1961), by the Federation of American Societies for Experimental Biology (1966), and by Bainbridge, Evans, and Rackham (1966). Methods in the social sciences are discussed by, for example, Ferber and Verdoorn (1962), Gibson, Hildreth and Wunderlich (1966), and Dubin (1969). Experienced scientists are aware of the sources of such information and the neophyte researcher should seek advice about such sources when planning a study.

NONSTATISTICAL PROCEDURES

Great stress has been given in this chapter to statistical procedures because of the benefits of studying a sample of a population rather than a single individual. Yet our discussion would be incomplete without mention of other useful procedures.

Case Studies

The case study is a time-honored method of acquiring insight into the working of the natural world. Whether we are interested in a species or plant or the structure of a human organization, it is almost always helpful to begin by becoming familiar with one individual from the group. This study procedure is appropriate whenever little is known about the groups, or when detailed description of one case is the most efficient way for the scientist to acquaint himself with an organism or process he hasn't studied before. Or it may be the only feasible way to test a theory about an organization, for example. Such descriptive study procedures are common in studying life histories of organisms or organizations in entomology, ecology, or sociology.

Case studies almost always are a stepping-stone and are not structured beforehand. The researcher lets initial observation suggest additional factors to measure or tests to perform. Once a case study has provided sufficient insight, it is appropriate to develop a study that will reveal more about the population as a whole. This ordinarily will mean quantitative methods involving statistics.

Deductive Procedures

When scientists look at the real world, they must look either at a single individual (case study) or a sample (statistical study). Some research, however, deals entirely with models. Examples are economic theory, theoretical physics, and statistical theory. Useful things can be learned about most subjects simply by logically deducing conclusions from the specified model. Holling's (1966) paper, "The Functional Response of Invertebrate Predators to Prey Density," is an excellent example of how deductive methods in forest entomology may be effectively coupled with direct experimental observation.

Such analytical methods of deduction are highly developed in formal logic and mathematics and cannot be covered here. Simulation, however, is another deductive method—one that electronic computers have made useful. A process, either mental or physical, or a product, is imitated or simulated by a model. The model may be iconic if the simulation is a "pilot plant" trial of a new production process or, at the other extreme, the model may be completely symbolic. Consequences of the model are deduced by a highly structured, trial-and-error manipulation of the model, rather than by purely deductive logic.

A specified model may be tested internally rather than against the real world. This kind of experimentation can be based on simulated observations rather than on direct observation of actual phenomena. For example, "outcome" may be recomputed repeatedly, based on all possible combinations of "input" variables. This provides a test of the sensitivity of "outcome" to changes in the values of "input" variables and, therefore, a measure of the relative importance of these determinants. The model may give clearly unrealistic responses in certain ranges of values for "input" variables, which would indicate that the model needs to be modified or its domain limited. This kind of simulation provides an empirical check on the deductive validity of a model. Various study procedures involving simulation have been developed for a wide range of applications. An introduction to this burgeoning subject can be gained from *Computer Modeling and Simulation* (Martin 1968).

Developmental Procedures

In earlier chapters we have indicated that some resource management problems will lead to study objectives that involve development of a process, a service, or product. This kind of study, which ordinarily falls in the research and development category, is most common in manufacturing industries. Study procedures for such objectives are highly specialized in some areas of technology (*e.g.* pulp and paper industries) and much less structured in others (*e.g.*, regional planning). The procedures will often be a unique composite of deductive procedures, particularly simulation, designed experiments, case studies, and trial and error. Because of this variety, we are unable to specify procedures useful to a wide range of readers. A search of the literature appropriate to a specific application should assist the beginning researcher. The more highly structured developmental studies are most subject to efficient, problem-oriented planning such as discussed, for example, by Ackoff (1962), Lloyd (1966), Lyden and Miller (1967), and Sandretto (1968).

REFERENCES

ACKOFF, R. L. 1962. Scientific method. Wiley, N. Y. 464 p.

ANDREWARTHA, H. G. 1961. Introduction to the study of animal populations. Univ. of Chicago Press, Chicago. 281 p.

BAINBRIDGE, R., G.C. EVANS, and O. RACKHAM. 1966. Light as an ecological factor. In proc. British Ecol. Soc. Symposium 6, Cambridge, England. Wiley, New York. 464 p.

BLALOCK, H. M., Jr. 1964. Causal inferences in nonexperimental research. Univ. of North Carolina Press, Chapel Hill, N. C. 200 p.

BLISS, C. I. 1967. Statistics in biology, Vol 1. McGraw-Hill, N. Y. 558 p.

BROSS, I. D. J. 1953. Design for decision. Macmillan, N. Y. 276 p. Free Press Paperback Edition, 1965.

COCHRAN, W. G., and G. M. COX. 1957. Experimental designs 2d ed. Wiley. N. Y. 611 P.

COHEN, M.R. 1944. A preface to logic. H. Holt, N.Y. 209 p. (reissued in 1956, Meridian Books)

CONANT, J. B. 1951. Science and common sense. Yale Univ. Press, New Haven, Conn. 344 p.

DEMING, W. E. 1965. Principles of professional statistical practice. Ann. Math. Stat. 36(6):1883-1900.

DRAPER, N. R., and H. SMITH. 1966. Applied regression analysis. Wiley, N. Y. 407 p.

DUBIN, R. 1969. Theory building. Free Press, N. Y. 298 p.

FEDERATION OF AM. SOC. EXP. BIOLOGY. 1966. Environmental biology. Philip L. Altman and Dorothy S. Dittmer, Eds. Federation of Am. Soc. Exp. Biology; Bethesda, Md. 694 p.

FERBER, R., and P. J. VERDOORN. 1962. Research methods in economics and business. Macmillan N. Y. 573 p.

FESTINGER, L., and D. KATZ. 1953. Research methods in the behavioral sciences. Dryden Press, N.Y. 660 p. (reissued in 1966, Holt, Rinehart and Winston)

GIBSON, W. L., Jr., R. J. HILDRETH, and G. WUNDERLICH, eds. 1966. Methods for land economics research. (Collection of papers by several authors.) Univ. of Nebraska Press, Lincoln, Neb. 242 p.

HACKING, I. 1965. Logic of statistical inference. Cambridge Univ. Press, London. 232 p.

HILL, H. M., and R. H. BROWN. 1968. Statistical methods in chemistry. Analy. Chem. 40(5):376R-380R.

HILLIER, F. S., and G. J. LIEBERMAN. 1967. Introduction to operations research. Holden-Day, San Francisco. 639 p.

HOLLING, C. S. 1966. The functional response of invertebrate predators to prey density. Memoirs of Entomological Soc. of Canada. 48. 86 p.

JOHNSTON, J. 1963. Econometric methods. McGraw-Hill, N. Y. 300 p.

KEMENY, J. G. 1959. A philosopher looks at science. D. Van Nostrand, Princeton, N. J. 273 p.

KEMPTHORNE, O. 1952. Design and analysis of experiments. Wiley, N. Y. 631 p.

KISH, L. 1965. Survey sampling. Wiley, N. Y. 643 p.

LLOYD, L. E. 1966. Techniques for efficient research. Chemical Pub. (dist. Tudor) New York. 215 p.

LYDEN, F. J., and E. G. MILLER. 1967. Planning, programming, budgeting: a systems approach to management. Markham, Chicago. 443 p.

MARTIN, F.F. 1968. Computer modeling and simulation. Wiley, N.Y. 331 p.

MOSBY, H. S., ed. 1963. Wildlife investigational techniques. 2d ed., rev. Wildlife Society, Wash., D. C. 419 p.

NEWMAN, D. W. 1965. Instrumental methods of experimental biology. Macmillan, N. Y. 560 p.

OSTLE, B. 1963. Statistics in research, 2d ed., Iowa State Univ. Press, Amer, Iowa. 585 p.

PLATT, J. R. 1964. Strong inference. Science 146:347-353.

SALTER, L.A., Jr. 1948. A critical review of research in land economics. Univ. of Minn. Press, Minneapolis, Minn. 258 p. (reissued in 1967, Univ. of Wisconsin Press)

SANDRETTO, P. C. 1968. The economic management of research and engineering. Wiley, N. Y. 199 p.

SIEVER, R. 1968. Science: observational, experimental, historical. Am. Scientist 56(1):70-77.

VAN NORMAN, R. W. 1963. Experimental biology. Prentice-Hall, Englewood Cliffs, N. J. 243 p.

WHITEHEAD, A.N. 1925. Science and the modern world. New American Library, N.Y. 191 p.

WILLIAMS, E. J. 1959. Regression analysis. Wiley, N. Y. 214 p.

WILSON, E. B., Jr. 1952. An introduction to scientific research. McGraw-Hill, New York. 373 p.

WOLINS, L. 1967. The use of multiple regression procedures when the predictor variables are psychological tests. Educ. and Psych. Measurement 27(4):821-827.

A PROBLEM ANALYSIS
IMPACT OF RECREATION ON
TIMBER MANAGEMENT

7
PREPARING
WRITTEN STUDY PLANS

The next step in study planning is preparing a written study plan. In this chapter we consider *why* it is useful to *write* a study plan and *what* to record in one, briefly retracing the framework of study planning.

The written study plan reflects all the thinking and preparation discussed in the previous steps. Hence, in preparing a written study plan, the researcher refers to and records from his mental or written outline of the previous processes. He has already studied the pertinent literature in the process of study planning, and cites this where appropriate in the body of the study plan. A separate "literature review" section is not likely to serve a useful purpose in a study plan.

FUNCTIONS OF WRITTEN STUDY PLANS

By writing a plan you assure yourself that the study is well planned, carefully thought through, and fully understood before beginning to collect data. Ideas are usually not clear until they have been refined by the rigor of writing them down. Only in written form can we see the full relationship of the parts. Writing shows the fuzziness of what on purely metal reflection seemed clear.

When the details are written, you can get suggestions from other specialists. This helps avoid costly errors of many kinds. Having a written plan is the only way to obtain sound assistance from statisticians and other specialists. Communicating accurately in a brief conversation is difficult, and remembering what is said is even more difficult. A written plan provides a permanent record and ready reference.

A written study plan will help you execute your study and your report. It will simplify the collection and analysis of data, and make it feasible for such work to be carried out by supporting personnel. A written plan will make it simpler to revise procedures, to record revisions, and later relate them to the data.

Because a written plan enables others to see what the study will be, the plan will also help you to obtain assistance in conducting the study. Seeing and understanding the study plan, other agencies may be encouraged to provide financial support, facilities, equipment, field or laboratory assistants, and other specialists. The written plan allows you to make estimates of time requirements and costs, and to check these with researchers who have had greater experience. You can size up available resources and decide what assistance to seek.

If you have a written plan, you can coordinate your study more effectively with other studies. And a very important advantage of a written study plan is that it permits continuity of research in spite of personnel changes. The study can go on. This protects the investment that you and the supporting organization have made in the study.

ITEMS TO INCLUDE

Listed below are nine items we suggest be included in every study plan. These, of course, need not be the headings nor the outline of the plan; the form of study plans will vary greatly. These items may, however, provide a checklist to consider.

Abstract
The abstract should quickly orient the reader and summarize the study for him. It should briefly define the problem, study objectives, the scope of the study, the study design, and the form of analysis.

Summary of Problem Analysis and Project Plan
A concise statement is needed to show how this study relates to the problem it is to help solve, and how it ties into related studies. To do this you must specify the problem, indicate its importance, and show how the information provided by this study will help solve the problem. If there is a project plan under which this study will be executed, it too should be summarized, with the summary indicating how this study *relates* to the project and to the other studies planned as a coherent attack on the problem.

Statement of Objective

We have seen how the study objective determines the form of analysis, study design, and methods of observation. And we have seen how important it is to have an objective that can be achieved by study planning. Stressing a single primary objective leads to better training and practice. If secondary objectives are planned, however, it is necessary to identify them as secondary, and to explain why they are included. For secondary objectives that require additional observations, it may be simpler to write separate plans.

Usually you will want to provide first a general statement of objectives, one that involves factors or incompletely specified variables. Then the objective can be restated in specific terms of the subject matter and application. Finally, where statistical methods are involved, the objective should be stated in statistical terms.

For the specific statement of objectives, the following are needed:

(a) Definition of specific information to be provided, and whether qualitative or quantitative. If a relationship is to be quantified or tested, identify the specific dependent and independent variables.

(b) Statement of whether an objective evaluation of validity of estimate or inference is required; if it is, how precise must the estimate be and how small a difference between treatments do we wish to detect?

(c) Statement identifying and describing the population to which the resulting information is to apply.

(d) If a relationship is involved, whether users of results will wish to predict single values of the dependent variable or to estimate changes in the dependent variable associated with changes in the independent variable.

Variables and Sources of Variation

The study plan should contain a detailed description of the variables and sources of variation involved with reasons for choosing particular variables.

First, specify the dependent variable in detail. Include a discussion of the other variables that could have been used within the problem analysis and study objective, and why this particular one was selected.

Next, list all potentially important sources of variation (factors) that might cause the dependent factor or variable to vary. For each source of variation state how it will be handled in the study. Each could be

(a) regarded as a treatment, to be measured or controlled; or

(b) regarded as a covariate, to be measured so as to improve the sensitivity of the study and aid in interpretation; or

(c) averaged over or separated out in the study design (*i.e.* by randomization or restrictions in design); or

(d) disregarded as minor.

And finally, specify the independent variable that is selected to quantify each factor or source of variation. Consider explaining why particular variables were chosen to quantify particular factors, and discuss how well you think the variables do the job. Your reasoning can then be clarified and subjected to review. Units and scale of measurement (*i.e.*, logarithmic vs. arithmetic scale) influence interpretation and use of results, so this makes it important to explain why particular units will be used. Also, you must justify the level of precision selected for making measurements. And it is useful to record whether the variables are continuous or discrete, quantitative or qualitative, and if a choice was possible, why one or the other was chosen.

Planned Analysis and Study Design

If the study objective leads to collecting data, it will lead also to some form of analysis and some particular study design to enable this analysis. This will often require a statistical analysis to enable inferences to be made on a probability basis; this in turn will involve a statistical study design—either sampling design or experimental design. The analysis is critical for satisfying most of the study objectives that arise from the approach we have considered, and, hence, so is the study design.

The study plan should justify and record the anticipated analytical procedures, and the study design that will give rise to the appropriate data. These sometimes are placed in an appendix.

As a first step, state the study objective in statistical terms, including the relevant details of the statistical model, the assumptions, parameters to be estimated, and hypotheses to be tested. Next, specify the form of the analysis. Consider the relevant assumptions for this form of analysis and indicate how they will be met, or wherein they won't. For example, if an analysis of variance is involved, you should present the analysis-of-variance table, listing sources of variation, degrees of freedom, and mean-squares. The plan should include a discussion of the specific inferences and interpretations to be drawn from different outcomes of the study, and of any sequential procedures of estimating or testing.

The study plan should also describe the study design—how samples will be taken or experiments arranged. This will include details about such things as layout, size of plots, width of isolation strips, definition of sampling or experimental units, confounding procedures, and description of the region, area, or group of things that will constitute the population to be sampled.

The number of samples or size of experiment planned should be justified. The number depends on, and must be formally related to:

(a) precision required in estimate or difference to be detected (alternatively, the value of additional precision may be compared with sampling costs)

(b) level of confidence, or level of significance

(c) variability of study material

(d) cost of sampling or experimental observation, and

(e) number of strata, blocks, etc., and method of allocating units to strata blocks, cluster, stages, etc.

Field, Laboratory, and Computational Procedures

The study plan should include relevant details about methods of handling or treating experimental material; field or study layout, location and orientation; controlling treatments and study environment (apparatus, etc.); taking measurements, observations, photographs; and making computations.

It will be useful to indicate the data collecting and processing equipment that will be used. For example, electronic recorders and electronic computers will influence the form of data collection tallies and the form of computations. If a computer is to be used, the study plan should indicate whether programs are available or must be written. If programs are to be written as a part of the study, then details should be recorded in an appendix. Detailed instructions that relate to field or laboratory procedures, and design of apparatus may best be put in an appendix too—along with recording forms and data processing programs and procedures.

Describe these procedures in sufficient detail so that any new research man with a suitable background could take over and carry out your study with little or no verbal instruction.

Plans for Reports and Publications

One of the most important functions of the researcher is to communicate the results of his study to the people who can use it in solving their problems. A study is not finished until this phase is also completed. Consequently, in planning your study you must anticipate this activity, plan it, and schedule it. The study plan should include a list of the reports and publications that will be necessary to communicate the results to the appropriate readers. Each group of readers should be described and its potential use of the results outlined. This will lead to a suggested medium for publication and a brief description of the reports and publications themselves.

Requirements, Schedule, Assignments

So that the researcher and his sponsoring agency may plan for financial support and make physical arrangements, the study plan must include a detailed schedule of manpower, time, and money required.

The plan should show personnel requirements, giving separate estimates of man-days of professional vs. subprofessional work for each of the following phases: preparing study plan; establishing the study (laying it out, setting up apparatus, applying treatments, etc.); collecting the data; analyzing and interpreting the results; preparing the final reports; and preparing the publications.

Prepare a list of major equipment and facilities needed; identify what is now available and what must be acquired. This list might include such things as greenhouse space, laboratory space, land (soil types, vegetation), spectrophotometers or other special analytical equipment, data processing services and equipment, and contracted laboratory analyses. For each item include a statement of how much is required, how much it will cost, where it can be obtained, and how long it will be needed.

Prepare a timetable or schedule that shows when each phase of the study will be carried out. This is best arranged according to the same categories and phases used to show personnel requirements.

Your study plan should also show assignments of responsibility for each phase of the study, and show sources of personnel, financial support, equipment, and facilities. If cooperators from outside the main supporting agency are working, then their responsibilities should be made clear too.

Appendix

The appendix should contain all those materials and details relevant to the study plan and its execution, but not essential to communicate the essence of the study plan. The appendix ordinarily includes such materials as literature cited; tally sheets; recording forms; formats of punched cards; detailed instructions for field, laboratory, or computational procedures; diagrams and specifications of special apparatus; examples of computations or equations on which computations will be based; computer programs; flow charts, etc.; and relevant maps and sketches.

NECESSITY FOR REVIEWS

The study plan is not complete until it has been reviewed and all suggested modifications considered. An important reason for preparing a written study plan is to obtain the advice of others before beginning the study. It also provides the supporting foundation or agency opportunity to approve the whole plan thus assuring you that it will support the study to its completion. Such reviews might also provide a valuable form of communication between a Ph.D. candidate and his committee as to the adequacy of proposed dissertation research.

This is the first critical phase in the research activity where review is necessary—before the data are collected and before it is too late to improve the plan and thus avoid disastrous mistakes. The second critical phase for review is in the preparation of publications for communicating the results—the importance of this is treated in Chapter 9. Review of the study plan, however, will help to assure you will have something worthwhile to communicate. After the study is completed, no amount of good writing can save the day if there is nothing important to communicate because either the study objective was not good, or was not achieved.

By seeking reviews, you can get the advice of well-informed and experienced colleagues to help you improve your understanding of the problem; to choose the most important study objectives; and to select procedures for efficiently achieving these objectives. This is the kind of insurance no researcher wants to be without. Therefore, you should have your study plan carefully reviewed, and revise the plan in accordance with such good advice as you can get.

You then can initiate the study with the best plan that can be devised at that time. As the study proceeds, more will be learned and it will be necessary to further amend the study plan. These written amendments then become a part of the study plan.

8

MAINTAINING ESSENTIAL RESEARCH RECORDS

Objectivity is fundamental to scientific methodology. But objective evaluation of research findings can result only from well-documented studies. The researcher's memory, quite unintentionally, selectively retains certain facts but allows others to escape. And research results are frequently needed by researchers other than the one who collected them. Thus, record keeping is an integral part of the researcher's job.

Scientists have long placed great emphasis on complete and accurate recording of the conditions, methods, and results of research. Yet this skill often has been learned haphazardly—by trial and error. The novice may keep incomplete records of his research activities because he feels that record keeping is an unproductive chore. But many costly observations have been repeated because records were inaccurate or incomplete. Similarly, the results of a study may be misinterpreted, even uninterpretable, for lack of good records. On the other hand, the researcher who revels in records finds little time for anything else. His unnecessary records, and records kept in unnecessary detail, do not facilitate research.

Good records seldom occur by accident; they are planned. Their format and content should be specified in the study plan; this is particularly true for data records. Future uses of the records must be anticipated and the records designed to satisfy those needs. The researcher should always be alert for better record-keeping techniques, however, and should modify the study plan when improved records can result. Attention to such detail is essential for efficient research.

All records should have certain attributes. First, records should be accurate and complete. These two attributes are attained by deciding beforehand what to record and how to record it and by adhering to these decisions. Second, all records should be permanent enough to remain intact and legible as long as they will be needed. This is of special concern in field research where record keeping sometimes is made more difficult by adverse weather (Bradley and Denmead 1967). Third, records should be easy to file and to retrieve. This means that each separate sheet or card must contain a statement that identifies the study, the type of information, when and where it was taken, and by whom (Williams 1965; Janda 1968). Finally, every record should be understandable by itself, or with a minimum of reference to plans or instructions. Excessive and nonstandard abbreviations, and failure to define terms adequately, are common sources of trouble here.

The purpose of this chapter is to point out the many different uses of research records and how these uses dictate the essential characteristics of records. Occasionally, use requirements may conflict and you will need to decide which characteristics best suit the combined needs (Bourne 1963).

OBTAINING STUDY RESULTS

An important function of such research records as the study plan and amendments to it, standard laboratory procedures, data compilation and analysis procedures, and computer programs is to describe in detail the methods to be followed (*and* those that *were* followed) in obtaining the study results.

The importance of such records can be appreciated by considering who will collect the data. Often you will either completely or partially delegate this responsibility to a technician or data analyst. A computer will do only what it is told; technical assistants may too but, in the absence of explicit instructions, they may also proceed to collect and analyze data by a self-determined method. The research planner must communicate to his field and laboratory assistants every necessary detail about how to make the observations—what, when, and how to observe; the format of the records; how to prepare the data for analysis; instructions for transcribing them to punched cards or magnetic tape; and what specific analyses or compilations to perform.

The study plan is your main procedure report. Its function and content are described in detail in Chapter 7. But frequently, as a study proceeds the plans are changed; a new sampling plan must be selected, additional measurements are found necessary, and so on. Such changes in the formal study plan are documented by amendments which should refer to the appropriate section of the study plan, present the new plan, and describe the reasons for change. The need to communicate with other participants in a study reinforces the requirement of permanently recording changes in the study plan.

Tally forms, photographs, drawings, maps, and computer input media (punched cards or magnetic tape) are special data records used for observational information. Tally forms sometimes provide for repeating or otherwise verifying measurements, and usually contain space for recording unusual or unexpected conditions and occurrences. The information from tally forms that have been designed to ease data collection is sometimes transferred to punched cards or other special records designed to facilitate compilation and analysis.

Records of computational procedures are often used to organize and facilitate mathematical analyses. Special computational forms should identify the analytical purpose of the computations, and the specific method to be employed. Some forms show a computational process step-by-step, indicating the source of inputs at each step and the mathematical operation to be performed, reminding the analyst of the steps he must follow, and helping him to be accurate and complete. Computer programs constitute a similar record, because they too specify a step-by-step analytical process.

INTERPRETING THE RESULTS

No study is complete until the results have been interpreted and the interpretations communicated to the clientele identified by the problem analysis. Interpretation of research results is difficult, but particularly so if the records of the study are inadequate; if they do not have the attributes described previously. The format of a record—whether it be a report, a tally sheet, a punched card, magnetic tape, picture, or graph—is important to research efficiency.

The interpretation of study results may involve every record that has been prepared during the study. The need for the study plan and all other procedure reports is obvious. But elaborate experimentation often requires documentation beyond that found in the study plan. Materials reports for laboratory experiments or plot-establishment reports for field research are examples of such records. They may describe the samples or individuals used in the study, deviations from measurement procedures, unusual treatments and/or responses, and any other conditions or occurrences that seem germane.

Records of both the original and processed data are the basis for interpretations. Thus their format is critical. Graphs and charts are designed to communicate trends, differences, or specific functional relationships illustrated by the data. Or the data may be summarized in tabular form. In addition, drawings, maps, and photographs may be needed. Pictorial data record much information, but such records are not selective and are seldom amenable to precise analysis.

Occasionally, even the original data must be reconsulted. And of course this will be easier if they are readily accessible, as when they are on computer cards or tapes. If large quantities of data are involved in a study, electronic data processing should be considered. This allows rapid sorting for examination of specific portions of the data, in addition to the computational advantages. Moreover, tables or graphs can be produced automatically as the final step in electronic computation.

Abstract cards are a common special data record used to compile existing knowledge and experience (Scheele 1961; Loosjes 1967). They will permit comparisons of your study results with previous information on the subject. Abstract cards usually contain a citation to identify the source of the information, an abstract of the relevant information, and a reference to a classification system by which they can be rapidly sorted. A punched card format sometimes is useful because it allows a single card to be classified in many different ways.

PROVIDING ADMINISTRATIVE CONTROL

A researcher seldom funds his own research. Instead, his financial support is obtained through his employer or a contract or grant from a corporate, philanthropic, or governmental agency. Industrial research is directly funded within the corporate structure. In any event, those who pay for the research have a right, and will exercise it, to know what research will be done or has been done with their money. These agencies retain control over the research and make administrative decisions based on what is communicated to them in various administrative reports.

Research reports are also used to develop long-range plans. A wood-processing company may plan new research if current research progress appears profitable, or it may even plan to produce a new product. On a large scale, reports of the initiation or progress of individual studies are compiled to provide a national research inventory such as the Current Research Information System (CRIS). Such inventories allow agencies responsible for national planning to compare our total research effort with long-range needs.

Reporting systems such as CRIS also allow research planners to determine what related research is being or has been done. And they provide information that permits further communication directly with those researchers.

Administrative reports are of several types. The research prospectus or the project plan is intended to obtain permission to initiate new research. Progress reports, annual reports, or status reports specifically relate what has been accomplished during some period and what will be accomplished during the next. Significant findings, personnel involved or needed, cooperative arrangements, manuscripts prepared, and reasons for deviation from previous plans are usually included.

When the study is completed, a termination, "office," or summary report is prepared. It is designed to bring together under one cover the content (in abbreviated form) of the study. It serves as a permanent and detailed reference source for the study, and is frequently employed as a terminal report when no publication of study results is planned. The summary report should include such topics as an abstract of the problem analysis, the contribution of past research, the study objectives, study approach, methods, materials, results, and interpretations.

Administrative reports of all types provide the link between the researcher and various people outside a study. They must communicate the significant contribution of a study clearly but concisely. Some specific facts may be reported, but the researcher is judged by, and rewarded for, his ability to sort out the valuable information and report it only.

AFTER COMPLETING THE STUDY

Selected records of a completed research project should be retained for review and subsequent analysis by other researchers as well as persons having proprietary interests in them. These research records are valuable for planning future research and as a source of data for future use.

By the time a study is completed, the researchers involved usually have discovered ways by which the study could have been improved. Suggested improvements are an essential part of a termination report; later, these suggestions are invaluable to researchers planning subsequent or related studies. In addition, past study plans and procedure reports are a source of ideas for the research planner. And the results provide estimates of population variances, means, and coefficients in relationships—necessary data for the design of efficient experiments.

After a researcher has published his findings he may feel that the original data are of no further use and may be destroyed. Rarely is this so. If the study was integrally related to other studies associated with a significant problem, the data may be valuable later. Other researchers may wish to initiate a related study and assimilate into it the data from your study, particularly when data collection is expensive. Or you may wish to reevaluate your data in light of the subsequent findings of your own or others. And some studies, such as resource surveys, are intended to provide data continuously for numerous other studies and analyses. The traditions of objective scientific inquiry dictate that a researcher make his data available to others once he has received proper credit for his work (Wolins 1962).

Research records should be available to others for several additional reasons. If the research was performed under contract to some public or private agency, then the research records may actually become the property of the contracting agency. When research is paid for by public funds the research records are public property, and the public may rightfully insist on reviewing them at any time. Thus, such records must be retained. If you have invented a process or a product, patent rights should be claimed, either to protect proprietary interests or to preserve the public domain (when the research is sponsored by a governmental agency). Your records are a vital part of your claim (Forman, 1961). When a patent dispute develops, a research organization must verify its claims by producing documentary evidence that it was the first to conceive the disputed process or product.

Research publications are aimed at too large an audience and publication costs are too large to justify including all data. This means that the basic data and related documents must be housed elsewhere. But the permanent maintenance of such records presents difficulties. A frequent proposal is to establish data repositories analogous to, or in conjunction with, libraries; research records would be permanently maintained there, but would be available for study when needed (Becker and Hayes 1967). Federal research agencies do this. Most industrial organizations maintain their records similarly, but their proprietary rights preclude use by others. Long storage of many research records requires special consideration of record format. Filing and retrieval systems are essential. Microfilm is especially advantageous, being extremely compact and permanent.

Of course, not all research records are worth permanent storage. Some data are ephemeral so are of little use after a few years. Other data can be reproduced more readily than they can be stored. In general, however, the problem analysis, project proposal, study plan and other procedure reports, the original data, and the termination report should be retained. Remember, data are of no value without these supporting documents.

REFERENCES

BECKER, J., and R. M. HAYES, ed. 1967. National documents handling systems for science and technology. Wiley, N. Y. 448 p.

BOURNE, C. P. 1963. Methods of information handling. Wiley, N. Y. 241 p.

BRADLEY, E. F., and O. T. DENMEAD, ed. 1967. The collection and processing of field data. Interscience, N. Y. 597 p.

FORMAN, H. I. 1961. Patents, research and management. Central Book, N. Y. 650 p.

HOUKES, J. M., ed. 1966. Management information systems and the information specialist. In Proc. of Symposium, Purdue University, July 12-13, 1965. Krannert Graduate School of Industrial Administration, Lafayette, Ind. 138 p.

JANDA, K. 1965. Data processing—applications to political research. Northwestern Univ. Press, Evanston, Ill. 288 p.

———. 1968. Information retrieval—applications to political science. Bobbs-Merril, Indianapolis, Ind. 230 p.

LOOSJES, T. P. 1967. On documentation of scientific literature. Translated by A. J. Dickson. Butterworth, London. 165 p.

SCHEELE, M. 1961. Punch card methods in research and documentation—special reference to biology. Translated by J. E. Holmstrom. Interscience, N. Y. 274 p.

WILLIAMS, W. F. 1965. Principles of automated information retrieval. Business Press, Elmhurst, Ill. 439 p.

WOLINS, L. 1962. Responsibility for raw data. Am. Psychol. 17:657-8.

9

WRITING
FOR PUBLICATION

Thus far, we have emphasized the part of research that involves finding out something new but have said little about the other part, telling someone about it. The "telling" is an essential part because, as we have implied earlier, the best information is useless unless it is communicated to someone who can use it.

Nevertheless, when we are beginning our research careers we often feel that writing up our results in publishable form is an annoying interruption for the scientist—something that keeps us out of the woods or laboratory where we belong. But the fruits of research are publications, and the researcher's responsibility is not fulfilled until he has prepared publications based on his studies.

The researcher with experience and a reputation as a productive scientist will already have demonstrated that he has a firm grasp on the principles of good scientific writing so this chapter will not be necessary for him. On the other hand, we believe we may be able to help many beginning researchers by a candid and elementary "how-to-do-it" approach to writing for publication. This belief is based not only on our own experiences, but on what other editors and scientists have said about the importance of communication. Baker (1956), Duffield (1965), Lynch (1966), and Woodford (1967) have written for various audiences about aspects of the difficulties. Duffield cautioned "we seem about to reach the pass where written communication becomes a problem rather than the accomplishment that distinguishes man from his simian brethren." A casual reference to the letters to the editor of a journal like *Science* will show that many share Duffield's view that improved communication of research results is important. We now turn our attention to this endeavor, which too many of us, unfortunately, have tended to neglect.

Research communications take many forms and may include the various records and reports discussed in the previous chapter. In this chapter, however, we will be talking mainly about publications. To be sure, most of the principles that apply to preparing publications also apply to writing study reports, the major difference being that in-house reports are generally prepared for small, exclusive, and sympathetic audiences, whereas publications are exposed to the entire world.

Publications and file reports are different also because they are written for different purposes: a file report records details of an experiment; a publication communicates some specific information. The difference is clear in the verbs: in a file report you "record" but in a publication you "communicate." It is similar to the difference between a warehouse and a showroom. The purpose of a warehouse is to store things; the purpose of a showroom is to display things and make them readily available. Although both buildings may house the same kind of material, they are constructed and used in entirely different ways. So it is with office reports and publications: one is intended to store information; the other to make it readily available. Hence, their form, size, and appearance are different.

At the outset, the researcher must realize that what was adequate scientific writing twenty years ago is not acceptable now. Because of the the tremendous volume of information being published each year today's hapless reader cries out for better writing since he simply does not have the time or inclination to wrest information from poorly written material. Moreover, the potential audience for research results is much broader now than it used to be. Time was when researchers could get away with merely talking to each other, but with the greatly increased interest in land use, natural resources, and outdoor recreation, many a nonscientist is actively and legitimately interested in what researchers have to say.

More and more, the writer about research, like any writer, is competing for his reader's time. To be sure, each discipline has its captive audience, those harried few who are obliged to read everything that pertains to their own narrow field. But the vast majority are free to pick and choose what they will read. Obviously they are more likely to read and understand good writing than bad writing. So if a scientist wants to be read and to enjoy the esteem of his peers and clients he must learn to be a competent writer.

There is nothing mysterious about what "competent" scientific writing is: simply stated, it is clear, brief, and precise. To be *clear*, a writer must know exactly what he wants to say; to be *brief* requires cold-hearted, objective judgment; and to be *precise* means that the writing must be organized to accomplish a definite, predetermined purpose. We will elaborate these points as we go.

With this background then, let us consider seriously how to approach writing systematically.

GETTING READY

The first thing to talk about is planning. Poor planning is the chief cause of poor writing. Neglect this essential part of the job and you doom yourself from the start. You cannot prepare a good publication unless you know what you want to do before you begin to write. Many a researcher's efforts at writing plainly indicate that he plodded his way from introduction to conclusion with only a hazy idea of his purpose. Such manuscripts inevitably lack direction, unity, and coherence.

So get yourself thinking along the right lines before you even try to form an outline. Ask three pertinent questions: (1) What have I found? (2) What does it mean? (3) Who cares—and why?

What have I found? At first blush, this question may seem too elementary and self-evident to bother with. But before you impatiently brush it aside, try answering it. In one sentence, that is, and without using numbers. This can sometimes be an embarrassing question, but it must be answered before you try to write a publication. It is because some researchers are hard put to give a positive answer to this question that they often resort to the file-report style of presentation. They answer the question "What did I do?" instead of "What have I found?"

But a publication must communicate and not merely record, so it is plain that you must have the answer to "What have I found?" Until you answer it simply and directly, you're not ready to start writing. It doesn't matter whether you're writing a two-page note (I have found that it pays to put roofs on lumber piles) or a 200-page book (I have found how to manage northern hardwoods), you should be able to express your one big idea in one sentence. Don't try to go on until you can.

This does not mean that all your experiments have to provide a new method or theory before you can write about them. Sometimes "negative" information, such as that a certain treatment failed to produce the hoped-for results, is important in itself. This, as we discussed in Chapter 6, is something you found out and hence may be worth reporting.

What does it mean? Many of us are so afraid of making a mistake that we prefer merely to present the results of our experiments and let the reader draw his own conclusions. In doing so, however, we are shirking our main responsibility. Much of the work in laying out plots, collecting information, and even analyzing the data is just routine and can be done by a technician. The major areas where real professional experience and judgment are required are in planning research and in interpreting the results to decide what they mean. Professional timidity and scientific objectivity are not the same. No one is more qualified than the author to decide what his results actually mean. If he has conducted a sound experiment he should not be afraid to stake his reputation on the results.

Sometimes the answer to this question is obvious (It means that you had better roof your lumber piles.), but it is important that you put it into words anyway. This helps to set the limits and establish the goal of your manuscript.

Who cares? After you are satisfied that you really know what you found and what it means, the next thing to ask yourself is "Who cares?" This question may be easy to answer if the problem analysis and study plan are adequate. Some things, however, may have changed since the study plan was prepared so you will want to ask the question again. If somebody cares, decide who it is and why he cares. Then plan to write your publication to and for him.

The most important thing to keep in mind while you are writing a publication is that you're writing it for somebody else, and not for yourself. This means that you must consider the reader's viewpoints and interests before your own. It may be easy for you to present a certain bit of information in a certain way, but it may not be easy for your reader to receive it in that way. If so, it is you who must change—not the reader. You are writing for him.

Experience has shown that these three questions seldom can be answered offhandedly. The questions themselves seem simple, deceptively so, perhaps. But as we have implied, the answers may come hard. It is no disgrace to spend an hour or so, chin in hands, brooding over your answers, trying to distill them into one sentence each. You will find that it is worth it. Because during the distilling process you will have revealed to yourself the essence of your message. Now you're ready to write!

GETTING STARTED

As you begin writing, concentrate more on what you're saying than on how you say it. Let your mind run freely at this stage—put something down on paper! You will have plenty of time to worry about the niceties of language once you have that first draft in hand. That's why we talk about organization and content in this chapter and "being your own editor" in the next.

Write the title first. This is a natural sequel to "Getting Ready"; condensing your subject to a handful of words further helps your ideas to take form. Postponing it is a tacit admission that you do not yet know exactly what you are going to write about.

These suggestions should help you find a good title: make it short; put a verb in it; aim it at the reader; include "key words."

Make it short. A good title defines the subject precisely enough that the potential reader can decide whether he wants to read further, yet is brief enough that he absorbs the idea at a glance. Many scientific writers try to squeeze too much information into a title. You can tell the reader the details after you are sure he is listening. Short titles are appreciated by reader and librarian alike. The trick is to be brief without being too general. Be wary of the all-inclusive title that promises more than is really offered.

Put a verb in it. Titles with nouns, adjectives, and prepositions only are dead. No action; no sparkle. People like things that are alive, that move. So try to get some action into your title. The way to do this is to use verbs.

Show your reader how he fits into the picture. Tell him "YOU can do this" or "this means thus and so to YOU." Then he'll prick up his ears because you're talking about his favorite subject.

Computerized information retrieval is becoming common, so your title should contain the "key words" that will allow your publication to be plugged into the appropriate system. A little extra thought here will make your published work more readily available and hence more useful.

Of course, you will not be able to incorporate all these desirable characteristics into every title. But they do give you something to strive for. Here are some actual before-and-after examples:

Before: "A Photo Method for Recording Surface Defects on Standing Trees"

Contains several nonworking words: method, surface, standing.

After: "Recording Tree Defects in Stereo"

Wordage cut by half; "stereo" more descriptive than "photo."

Before: "A Comparison of Some Type Conversion Methods in the Missouri Ozarks"

Wordy, indefinite, obscure, dull.

After: "Increasing Forage on Ozark Wooded Range"

Shorter by nearly half, more precise and meaningful.

Before: "Some Economic Aspects of Improving Farm Woodlands"

The phrase "some economic aspects" is hackneyed and deadly and could allude to a hundred different things. The reader has begun to yawn already!

After: "Making Farm Woodland Improvement Pay"

Brief, but pointed, verb forms at both ends, the word "pay" is always an attention getter.

The "after" examples are shorter but all are more definite and hence more informative. They also all contain a verb form and so suggest something going on. All this adds up to more lively and appealing and hence more effective titles.

The introduction is an invitation. The next step is to write your introduction. This first paragraph or two is always the toughest part of a manuscript to write—even for the professionals. Here is where you win or lose your reader; here is where you find or lose yourself. Line for line, you will probably need to devote more time and effort to your introduction than to any other part of the manuscript. The question is, where do you start, and how?

Perhaps a homely analogy will help answer this and other questions as we go along. Pretend that, by means of your publication, you are going to take the reader on a trip. Your first task then is to persuade him to come, so word your invitation carefully and convincingly. Remember, he is a busy man, so tell him what he needs to know in a hurry.

Your "invitation" should answer three simple questions: Why? Where? and How?

Why are we taking this trip? The answer to this question explains the situation or describes the problem that justifies the publication; it defines the starting point.

Where are we going? Here you state the purpose of the publication. The purpose is generally to tell or to show something specific—*not* to report on a study. The difference is often so intangible as to exist mainly in the attitude or viewpoint of the author, but it is a significant difference nonetheless. Especially when the study did not turn out quite as expected or the information represents only part or a by-product of the study. The message you are trying to convey is the important thing; the study was merely the vehicle that brought you to this point.

How are we going to get there? You should tell the reader that what you have to say is based on some kind of study. This is a minor but sometimes overlooked point, but certainly you shouldn't start to describe your study until you have told the reader that you made one.

The above three points are the essential ingredients of the introduction. There is a growing trend also toward including a statement of the major results. Some writers rebel at this, feeling they are stealing their own thunder. Scientists should not be writing mystery stories, however. Their job is to keep the reader informed, not in suspense. If your guest knows from the start what he is going to find at the destination, what he sees along the way may have more meaning.

Of course, when you reveal your results at once, you put yourself on the spot. You commit yourself to a certain destination and so any deviation from a direct route from here to there will almost certainly be detected by the reader. You can't wander aimlessly around the countryside without arousing his impatience.

Just a word about literature reviews. In the past, it was common to review the literature in the introduction. But the practice was more traditional than logical. As Trelease (1958, p. 40) puts it: "the reader generally finds such a review dull, since he is not prepared so early in the paper to correlate past investigations with the specific problem in hand." Put any necessary references in those sections where they apply directly to your work. You will find that you will use fewer but they will work harder. Literature citations, like everything else in a manuscript, are to help convey the message; their purpose is not to prove that the author has done his homework.

Keep your introduction brief. You can usually say all that needs to be said in one or two paragraphs. A sentence or two may even be all the introduction needed to cover the elements just discussed. Sometimes you can kill one or two of these birds by implication. For example: "European alder proved to be promising for planting on strip-mine spoil banks." The situation is implied (the need for species suitable for spoil-banks), the purpose is implied (to help satisfy this need), and the source of information (research) is implied. The only thing plainly stated is the major finding or the message itself. All this in one sentence! The extent to which such subtleties can be used depends, of course, upon the subject matter and the intended reader. A professional forester acquainted with the strip-mine rehabilitation problem would grasp the meaning immediately. For the lay reader, on the other hand, the author would have to fill in the background—describe strip-mine spoil banks and explain why it is so hard to reforest them.

Often a more elaborate introduction is in order. An example is first paragraph from a publication by Brinkman, Rogers, and Gingrich, (1965):

> A basic objective of timber management is the maximum production of high-quality wood....The forester controls quantity and quality of timber yield by manipulating stand density between two extremes. In understocked stands, the average tree may grow fast, but total growth per acre will be low because all growing space is not utilized. Tree quality also may suffer. Conversely, in overstocked stands trees die because of crowding. The ideal stocking lies somewhere between. The question is: Where? In order to find out for shortleaf pine (*Pinus echinata* Mill.) in Missouri, we are studying the growth and yield in young stands thinned to five different densities. Our 10-year results are reported here.

The paragraph contains nine sentences, the first seven of which describe the situation and state the question. The authors begin with a very general statement, then immediately narrow the limits by getting to the density question in the second sentence. The stage setting is effectively completed in the seventh sentence with the one-word question "Where?" The eighth sentence mentions the study as the source of the information and the last one states the purpose of the paper. All elements are present, making this a good, complete introduction.

There can be no rigid formula for calculating how long an introduction should be. It is a matter of judgment, tempered by the principles given here. The best criterion is a simple one: Does the introduction adequately prepare the reader for what is to come? The extent to which the writer can evaluate his introduction from the reader's viewpoint will determine how well he will introduce his subject, how persuasive will be his invitation.

PACKING THE BAG

After you've told the reader where you're going to take him and why you're taking him there, the next thing to do is to provide him with the things he will need for the trip. In technical writing, this "baggage" consists of a description of your research procedures.

When you take a trip, your baggage may be important, but you don't travel just to carry baggage; you carry baggage because you're traveling. So it is with technical writing.

The study description is really only an incidental part of the publication; it is not the publication's reason for being. It has two functions, both of which support the main part of the manuscript: first, the procedures section should provide the reader with the qualitative information he needs to understand and interpret the results. This includes such things as a general description of the "guinea pig"—the object of study—and its treatment, plus any related information (location, site, climate, environment) that may have influenced the results. Second, this section should provide the quantitative information necessary to judge the validity of the results. This means the number, size, and arrangement of samples; the controls used; and the analytical procedures applied. On both counts, the criterion for deciding whether an item of information belongs in the procedures section is its direct bearing on the results. With this criterion in mind, here are some "don'ts" that should help you eliminate "excess baggage."

First, don't become so enthusiastic about packing the bag that you forget about the trip itself. We researchers often get carried away when we are telling what we did. This is understandable. The "doing" part of research is dear to our hearts; it is precisely describable, noncontroversial, and requires no interpretation—in short, it is matter-of-fact. This, then, is the part of the manuscript we feel most confident and comfortable writing. If we are sure of nothing else, we at least know what we did! But we deceive ourselves if we think that the reader is as fascinated by all this as we are. The writer must accept the fact that the reader is primarily concerned with the results; if the writer could have acquired the information adequately in any way other than by experiment, the reader would be just as satisfied. So what was done is not nearly so important as what was found.

Second, don't make your fellow traveler carry any more baggage than he needs; don't pack a steamer trunk if an overnight bag will do. Although you decide what goes into the bag, he is going to carry it. You don't want him to get so tired lugging it that he can't enjoy the scenery. So don't burden the reader with unnecessary details. For example, he will want to know that you measured 1,000 white oak trees, but he doesn't particularly care how you measured them unless, of course, you used some new or unusual tool or technique. The old idea that the study procedure must be described so completely that a reader could duplicate it himself is now obsolete. The great volume and broad audiences of research preclude this. And if that one-in-a-million reader does want to repeat your study, he can write you personally for the necessary information. Providing a satisfactory basis for that, you recall, is one of the functions of the written study plan.

Third, don't make the reader carry things throughout the whole trip that he can just as well pick up along the way. Too often we inadvertently waste a whole sentence in the procedures section with a statement like: "The trees were measured with a diameter tape to the nearest 1/10 inch 15 years after planting." This we can say less conspicuously and more naturally, when we present the results: "After 15 years the planted trees averaged 4.8 inches in diameter." Expressing diameter in tenths of an inch shows that the trees were measured that precisely. And it is immaterial that a diameter tape was used.

And finally, don't drag your reader over the same bumpy, zigzagging trail you followed when you were pioneering this route. Let him benefit from your experience. In other words, don't write it as you did it! Avoid the detours and dead-end roads that slowed you down; take him from here to there over the shortest, most direct route.

With these admonitions in mind, list all the facts and figures involved in setting up and carrying on the study. Examine each dispassionately and ask "Does this belong *here* ? Does it belong anywhere at all?" Cross out all that do not pass the test, arrange the rest in logical (not necessarily chronological) order, and you're ready to write your procedures section.

GETTING TO THE POINT

So far you have been dealing with preliminaries; invitations have been sent and bags packed. Now you're finally ready to travel—to talk about results and conclusions. This is the most important part of your publication, the reason for its being. Everything else has been leading up to this and hence is to subordinate to it.

Every astute reader asks two questions: What happened? and So what? Your results and conclusions are the answers to these questions.

Sometimes results and conclusions are best presented separately; other times it is more convenient to combine them. Your decision will be based chiefly on the amount and complexity of material to be discussed. For simplicity we will consider them separately.

Although your results were assembled and analyzed in quantitative terms and must to a certain degree be presented in quantitative terms, avoid the common tendency to drown your reader in statistics. A few well-chosen facts and figures will achieve more and be retained longer than a tubful of numbers. Begin your results section with a general statement that will mean something to the reader. Then, as necessary, support this statement with some appropriate figures. If, for example, your study evaluated the adaptability of several tree species to a particular site, start out with a clear declaration of what you found: "After 5 years, species D had the best survival and height growth." Avoid the temptation to begin with the survival percentages and height measurements of all species studied. And by all means don't start out by saying, "The results are summarized in table 1." These approaches put the burden of interpretation on the reader; you give him the figures and leave it up to him to sort them out and decide what they mean. This is the writer's job. The reader won't remember the numbers anyway; but he will remember the idea. Any child can name Everest as the highest mountain, but how many can tell you exactly how high it is? The idea is more important than the number!

Tables, charts, and illustrations should supplement, not complement, the manuscript. In other words, the narrative portion of your paper should stand on its own; tables and charts should only verify or elaborate points clearly made in the text (Larson 1958). To say it still another way, don't write so that you force the reader to interrupt his reading to look at a table or chart. Make it optional. Readers don't like to be interrupted. So tell your story in words, peppered with as few numbers as possible, and refer the interested reader to the more detailed numerical presentation in the tables and charts.

Don't just dump the results on the reader. Arrange them in some logical order so that each piece of information builds upon the preceding one. At the same time, spell out any trends or patterns in the results, no matter how obvious they may seem to you. Although you may be on familiar ground, the reader is a stranger to these parts and needs a guiding hand, especially when the road gets a little rocky.

It is easy to get cold feet just as you reach the climax of your paper—the conclusions. You may have planned and conducted a good tour through the introduction, procedures, and results. So when you're climbing that last hill to show the reader the view don't falter and stumble or turn back. You must bring yourself to say, "All this means thus and so."

All that was said when we discussed the question "What does it mean?" comes into focus at this point in the manuscript. This is where you tell the reader how the situation you described in the beginning has changed because of your research. Although by this time the conclusion may be self-evident, the reader likes to be reassured that his thinking coincides with yours. So climb that last hill, show him the view, and tell him what he is looking at. After all, this is what he made the trip for.

Here are some hints that will make the trip more pleasant and profitable for your guest as you guide him along the way.

Take the most direct route. Don't divert the reader's attention and waste his time by leading him off on various interesting (to you) side trips. Save these for another day (manuscript).

Gauge the route by your guest: if he is a novice without much background in this kind of travel, stick to the well-marked, paved roads; but if he has traveled this way before, if he is familiar with the subject matter, you can lead him into some roadless area as long as you follow a definite trail and don't just wander aimlessly around in the wilderness. But whatever you do, stay with him; don't run on ahead and leave him to find his own way.

A word about statistical methods. As you have seen from earlier chapters, the application of statistics may be essential in planning the study and in evaluating the results. But it should be treated with discretion in the publication. To be sure, the reader will want to know that appropriate statistical procedures were used throughout the study. But does he need the details about derivation of all your regression equations, and so on, and so on, to understand your major message? He will generally accept on faith that you know how to do these things. All you need do in most manuscripts is tell him that you did indeed do them and cite a standard reference for ordinary procedures. Statistics is not a magic wand; you know that these procedures cannot extract good information from a poor study, nor can they be used as a substitute for judgment. So don't blind your reader with a statistical smoke screen with the idea that this will take the place of good, sound reasoning.

GETTING STOPPED

The next hardest thing to getting started is getting stopped. Two extremes are common: the abrupt cutoff that leaves the reader hanging in midair, and the long, rambling fadeout that is sometimes repetitious, sometimes irrelevant. Avoid these extremes by taking him back to the starting point or at least to some familiar landmark, and by going back the way you came, not by some strange and devious route.

Whether you do your "stopping" at the end of the conclusions section or in a separate summary makes little difference. For short manuscripts—less than 10 typewritten pages—a summary is not always necessary; for longer papers a summary at the beginning or at the end is an accepted courtesy. Here the reader can either preview or review the trip.

Keep your summary brief. Don't rehash the whole manuscript. Remind the reader what you did and what you found. Don't use numbers unless absolutely essential. Leave your reader with your "big idea"—something he will remember and use.

WHERE TO GET FURTHER HELP

The neophyte researcher will have many specific questions when he prepares his first publications. We have not offered advice about many important details. For example, there will be questions about using literature citations, understanding and using proofreader's marks, correcting proof, preparing figures and illustrations, and setting up mathematical expressions. Such important but secondary matters are treated in many standard references for writers. You will want to have some of these available. Good ones include *Style Manual for Biological Journals* (Conference of Biological Editors, 1964), *A Manual of Style. (University of Chicago Press, 1968), and the U.S. Government Printing Office (1967) Style Manual*. Some learned or professional societies have authors' guides (*e.g.*, Hamilton *et al.* 1967), and scientific journals provide brief instructions for contributors.

Many excellent works on expository writing have been published. We consider Flesch (1949), Gunning (1952), Linton (1954), Kapp (1957), and Strunk (1959) to be among the best.

REFERENCES

BAKER, S. 1956. Scholarly style, or the lack thereof. Bull. Am. Assn. Univ. Professors 42(3):464-470.

BRAGG, L. 1966. The art of talking about science. Science 154:1613-1616.

BRINKMAN, K. A., N. S. ROGERS, and S. F. GINGRICH. 1965. Stand density affects yield of shortleaf pine in Missouri. U.S. For. Service Res. Paper CS-14.

BROWN, W. S., J. R. PIERCE, and J. F. TRAUB. 1967. The future of scientific journals. Science 158:1153-1159.

CONFERENCE OF BIOLOGICAL EDITORS. 1964. Style manual for biological journals, 2d ed. Am. Inst. Biol. Sci., Washington, D.C. 117 p.

DUFFIELD, J. W. 1965. Writing for a scientific or technical journal. J. Forestry 63:769-771.

HAMILTON, H. L., R. C. DINAUER, and S. MATTHIAS. 1967. Author's guide and style manual for Am. Soc. Agronomy, Crop Sci. Soc. Am., and Soil Sci. Soc. Am. Publications, Am. Soc. Agronomy, Madison, Wis. 40 p.

LARSON, E. vH. 1958. Tables for technical writers. Rev. Northeastern Forest Exp. Sta. 2, Paper 3, 45 p.

LYNCH, R. G. 1966. Linguistic barriers in science writing. BioScience 16(11):802-804.

UNIVERSITY OF CHICAGO PRESS. 1968. A manual of style. Univ. of Chicago Press, Chicago.

U.S. GOVERNMENT PRINTING OFFICE. 1967. Style manual (abridged). Rev. ed. Washington, D.C. 284 p.

WOODFORD, F. P. 1967. Sounder thinking through clearer writing. Science 156:743-745.

REFERENCES ON COMMUNICATING RESEARCH RESULTS

FLESCH, R. 1949. The art of readable writing. Harper, New York. 237 p.

GUNNING, R. 1952. The technique of clear writing. McGraw-Hill, New York, London. 289 p.

KAPP, R. O. 1957. The presentation of technical information. Macmillan, New York. 147 p.

LINTON, C. D. 1954. How to write reports. Harper, New York. 240 p.

STRUNK, W., Jr. 1959. The elements of style. Revised and enlarged by E. B. White. Macmillan, New York. 71 p.

TRELEASE, S. F. 1958. How to write scientific and technical papers. Williams and Wilkins, Baltimore. 185 p.

10

BEING YOUR OWN EDITOR

If you have followed all the suggestions in the previous chapter, you have by now a fairly complete, fairly well organized, fairly coherent rough draft. But you are far from having a finished manuscript. We have covered organization and content—now we're ready to talk about language.

Anyone can string words together, but this does not make him a writer, a communicator. A good writer must be a good self-editor. And self-editing is the hardest part of writing. Nearly every writer immediately falls in love with every word he sets down on paper. And it is heartbreaking to send your loved ones into exile. A first draft, no matter who the author, usually contains too many words, some wrong words, ambiguous words, double-meaning words, words that cannot be understood or can be misunderstood, plus a lot of just plain awkwardness. All this stands in the way of effective communication and so must be eliminated.

To write, you must be in a creative mood; to edit, you must be in a critical mood. So when you finish your first draft you've got to do some mental gear-shifting to get into the proper frame of mind. To make this easier, let your first effort cool for a week. Getting away for awhile will give a more objective attitude when you do return to it, and an objective attitude is what you will desperately need to be your own editor. If you've a good imagination, pretend you're editing someone else's work. This is much more fun. But by all means, train yourself to be ruthless, never give yourself the benefit of a doubt, and force yourself to justify every word.

Before you actually start to wield that blue pencil, you will want to dispense with a common bugaboo: style. The easiest way to dispense with it is to say "Don't worry about it—in fact, don't even *think* about it." Write naturally, be yourself, but don't consciously try to develop a writing style of your own. If you do it is almost sure to be stilted or showy. And certainly don't try to imitate someone else's style, no matter how much you may admire that person. Your style will take care of itself. A good style in scientific writing is inconspicuous; the message is the important thing.

Now, you're ready to be an editor, to put on your manuscript that final polish that makes your message crystal clear and instills confidence in the reader.

Here are a dozen specific faults common to mediocre writing. Eliminate these and you will have gone a long way toward making your manuscript clear, brief, and precise—which, you will remember, is what we said good scientific writing is.

Too few action verbs. Look at your verbs. Are most of them forms of the verb "to be" (is, are, was, were, has, have, had)? These are weak colorless words that just hang ideas in the air rather than push them along. A lazy statement like "has dominance over" transforms nicely to the more forceful "dominates."

Too many abstract nouns. Keep a sharp eye for excessive use of words ending in *ion, ment, ance, ence, ism.* These are abstractions, and while some of them are necessary, writers tend to wear them out. "Give consideration to..." whether you prefer that phrase to the more simple and direct "Consider..." Why "make recommendations on..." if you can "recommend..."? Ad infinitum.

Too many prepositions. It is easy to write a treatise that contains so many prepositions that if they were all printed in red the pages would look as if they had a severe case of the measles. Some prepositions are necessary, of course, but many can be eliminated by judicious revision. A little work on "Prior *to* the purchase *of...by* the State..." can dispose of all three prepositions as well as shorten and simplify the whole statement: "Before the State bought..."

These first three faults are complementary and interdependent. They generally go together. No matter which weakness you spot first, correcting it will automatically correct one or both of the others. Take a simple example: "We have a requirement for..." This partial sentence contains an abstract noun (requirement), an inactive verb (have), and a preposition (for). To eliminate an abstract noun convert it to an active verb. This invariably disposes of at least one preposition. So we wind

up with a shorter, livelier, and more direct statement: "We require..."
Try it. You will be surprised at how many places this will make an
immense improvement.

Too many adjectives and adverbs. If your manuscript contains an
overabundance of modifiers you are probably making one or more of
three mistakes: choosing the wrong nouns and verbs, being redundant,
or being overly cautious. The right noun, for example, can say as
much as a string of adjectives and say it much more effectively and
concisely. How about calling that "extremely large man" a "giant"?
Or that "excessively stingy man" a "miser"? And "small, preserved
cucumbers" are "pickles."

Watch out that you don't modify a noun with an adjective whose
meaning is inherent in the noun itself. Such obvious redundancies as
"round circle, steep cliff, and hollow tube" are often committed
absentmindedly and overlooked in haste.

And finally, avoid the tendency to dilute with unnecessary
qualifiers. If a thing is large, don't pussyfoot by saying "relatively
large." If you have successfully solved a problem, say so; don't try to
hide behind a timid "it is *apparently* successful."

Nouns used as adjectives. A widespread and growing disease is to
pile noun upon noun, one intended to modify, limit, or define the
other. We never seem to have showers anymore; it's always "shower
activity." Some of this, unfortunately, is unavoidable as new things,
concepts, and programs are invented and must be described. But much
of it is merely pedantry and can be eliminated by carefully searching
for the unnecessary words. Why say "management practices" when in
most cases you mean simply "management"? Why can't we say
"population" instead of "population level"? The good editor is
constantly on the lookout for unnecessary words.

Too few conjunctions. Conjunctions are connecting words, words
that tell how one idea is related to another. In effect, they tie the
manuscript together. Many writers fail to bind with conjunctions, so
their publications lack coherence. A judiciously placed *and, moreover,*
or *furthermore* alerts the reader that the statement to follow is adding
to or building upon the preceding one. On the other hand, a *but,*
however, or *although* indicates that one statement is going to subtract
from the strength or impact of another. Other connecting words and
phrases connote different relations between ideas, but they all
contribute to a smooth-flowing, comprehensible train of thought.
Their importance to effective writing cannot be overstated. In fact, if
the eight parts of speech were to be listed in their order of importance

in communicating ideas, conjunctions could well rank third behind verbs and nouns.

Too much passive voice. This self-inflicted malady, done in the noble name of objectivity, just about eliminates personal pronouns from a manuscript. This is its purpose: to be impersonal. Now why it is unscientific to say, "We measured the trees," is not clear, but you invariably see it written "The trees were measured." Nothing is ever done by persons, it just happens. Human hands are never allowed to sully these august proceedings. We scientists have been trying to kid each other like this for years. Aside from the fact that everyone knows some person measured those trees, the passive voice is not so natural to the English language as is the active. The "natural" way is to have the subject of a sentence *do* the acting, not be acted upon. A man would certainly not say to his wife, "You are loved by me." By the time she decided what he said, she would wonder if he really meant it! So forget about being "impersonal," write naturally—subject, verb, object. Of course you'll use the passive voice occasionally both for variety and convenience, but don't be shackled by it.

Indefinite antecedents. Pronouns mean nothing in themselves; they simply refer to some specific noun. Many writers trip up in their use of pronouns; they're careless; in some cases they give the reader no antecedent for a pronoun and in others they give him a choice of several. Take this sentence for example: "When the boys threw the rocks at the cans, they fell into the water." Who or what fell into the water—boys, rocks, cans, or all three? Here is a more realistic and actual example: "Although the oak wilt spores may spread through root grafts, they occur..." The reader thinks it is "grafts" that occur—but he can't be sure. You may alleviate this problem in two ways. Use the noun itself again instead of a pronoun. This removes all doubt, and a little repetition is better than a lot of uncertainty. The other way is to make the number of the pronoun agree with the number of its intended antecedent and disagree with the numbers of all other possible antecedents. This cannot always be done, however, so it is often best to completely recast the sentence.

Careless use of language. Scientists, generally meticulous about using numbers, can be extremely careless with words. Consider some actual examples. "Eight widely separated sources of eastern redcedar seed were planted in one nursery bed." This is such a common error that maybe you had to read it twice to see that the author says he planted "sources" when he means "seed." Sure, you may protest, he didn't say it exactly right, but you know what he means. In this case, yes; in others, no. If the man is either careless or inept with the language, doesn't this make you wonder whether these faults carry over into his research? He should have shunned the passive voice and started out, "We planted eastern redcedar seeds..." Here's another one: "Income from growing, harvesting, and processing timber would be strengthened." The words "income" and "strengthened" are incompatible—they just don't go together. Perhaps if the author had put the verb right after the subject where it belongs he would have said something like "increased" instead. Be sure the words you use say what you want them to say and that they belong together

Wordiness. It is axiomatic that a well-edited manuscript will be shorter than the original. Just how much shorter can be embarrassing to an inexperienced writer. You can vastly improve many manuscripts by striking out excess words. Read the following sentence through, except for the parenthetical words. *'Continued use of* (repeated) burning *as a management tool over a longer period of years* could *result in adverse effects on* (harm) both soil and vegetation."Now read it again, skipping the italicized words and adding those in parentheses. By deleting eighteen of the original twenty-four words while adding two (for a net reduction of two-thirds) we have a sentence that conveys the message (in context) better.

Be ruthless. It may hurt at first, but excess-word hunting can become a challenge.

Roundabout statements. Sometimes we seem to delight in saying things the hard way. Perhaps we're trying to convince readers that our story is more complex than it really is. If not, how could you account for a man writing (and one did), "noninfiltrated precipitation water" when (he sheepishly admitted) he meant "runoff"? The tendency to express everything in abstract terms is a strong one, but to communicate findings rather than embalm them, you must vigorously resist it.

Here's another delinquent: "The heights of the planted shortleaf pine and redcedar were positively related to the size of the opening where they were planted and, generally, to the freedom from hardwood competition." Immediately you see two things: the nondescript verb (were related) and the abundant prepositions (five of them). Result—a weak, cluttered sentence. Although the grammatical subject is "heights" (an abstraction), the author is actually talking about trees. And what he is saying about them is that the taller ones had more space and less competition than the smaller ones. So his use of the word "heights" is a backhanded way of referring to growth.

Now we see some light and suggest this: "Trees grew faster the larger the opening and the less competition from hardwood brush." The subject is a concrete object instead of an abstract concept, the verb is active and strong, only one preposition is left, and fewer than half the original number of words.

One more: "The more evident effects of burning were the earlier initiation of a vegetative growth and earlier maturity of individual plants." Here again note the subject and verb: "effects...were" An abstraction and a form of one of the weakest verbs in the language. Imagine that poor little, lifeless "were" trying to push that whole sentence along all by itself! Solution? First, find the real subject. We have to look a long way here, clear to the end of the sentence. There we discover he is talking about plants. Now for a verb. Are any of those nouns verbs in disguise? Three of them, at least—initiation, growth, and maturity. Simplify "initiation" to "began" and here's what we come up with: "Plants on burned areas began growing and matured earlier than on unburned areas." Shorter, livelier, clearer.

As you can see, roundabout statements can contain any of the previous eleven faults we have discussed. They are a real challenge to the writer-editor who created them. But overcoming them will make you a better writer, and even a better thinker.

Now that all the rough spots have been smoothed out and you can almost enjoy reading the paper yourself, go back over it and check to see that the title is appropriate, the introduction does indeed "introduce" the paper, you have made no promises at the beginning that you did not keep at the end, the procedures section is streamlined as much as possible, your paper does have a purpose and that purpose has been achieved, and you have left the reader with something definite and useful to remember.

11
FINAL THOUGHTS

We have constructed a framework for problem analysis and study planning and execution. We have provided advice about communicating the results of research. Many other matters, however, concern the young researcher as a new member of the scientific community. Though we cannot deal with all of these, a few warrant special mention.

One of these is the difficult and important matter of deciding who should be the author of a research publication. Another is the professional responsibility and ethics of critical review. This involves both providing technical reviews of study plans and publication manuscripts for your peers, and seeking such reviews of your own scholarly efforts. Finally, there is the broad area of scientific creativity and the human aspects of scientific endeavor. We should like to discuss each of these issues briefly.

AUTHORSHIP

Whose name should appear beneath the title? Who should be credited with authorship?

The dictionary defines author as "one who writes, a composer." But it also says "the originator, beginner, or creator of anything." Scientific tradition has included both concepts in defining what constitutes authorship. In scientific publications, authorship indicates who is primarily responsible for what has been found as well as for composing the report describing the discovery.

When research was largely a one-man venture, this question rarely arose. The researcher developed an idea, designed a study to test it, conducted the study, and then wrote a paper describing the results. Obviously he was listed as author—the only author. But today much research is conducted by a multi-disciplinary team of scientists, and one publication may report the results of two or more studies conducted by different individuals. One person may begin a study and another complete it and report the results. Obviously, the correct answer to the authorship question is not always simple.

The question is an important one, however. Research is like an iceberg—most of it is not visible, even to your professional colleagues. But its value and importance must be judged from what is visible—and in research this is the final publication. Every scientist's reputation is largely determined by the significance, quality, and number of publications that bear his name—particularly those that list his name as senior author (Shaw 1967). Grants, promotions, salaries, and other forms of professional recognition depend on the scientist's name being associated with publications that describe the work for which he is responsible.

The difficulty lies then in knowing who to include as authors, and who to list first as senior author. Unfortunately, scientific traditions have not been sufficiently codified to provide a clear basis for answering these questions, but some guidance is possible.

The person who actually prepares the publication manuscript is always listed as an author. Usually he is listed as senior author. The senior author will receive major credit, recognition, and blame for the publication and for the discovery it reports. For this reason, if authorship is to acknowledge the contributions of more than one researcher, primary responsibility should be decided before writing, and the writing should be assigned to that person.

Who else has contributed to the discovery being reported? For large studies, the list includes dozens of people, sometimes hundreds. To name a few—the persons who: first put into words the basic idea the study is reporting, who suggested the study, who wrote the study plan, who laid out the statistical design and the method of data analysis; plus those who collected the data, those who processed and analyzed it, and those whose manuscript reviews suggested new insights that significantly modified the conclusions. We cannot omit the editor who made major changes in the manuscript; and so on.

Obviously, not all these contributions can be acknowledged by authorship. By custom, some of this assistance is not acknowledged in print. This includes the contributions of technicians or researchers who collect the data, the computer specialists who processed it, the typists, and the printers. It is not that their contributions are less important, it is simply that authorship is not the way their contributions are customarily acknowledged.

Acknowledgment of unusual technical assistance may be noted in a preface, foreword, or footnote. This is a nice courtesy, but such acknowledgments are not the stuff out of which professional reputations are built. Major scholarly contributions are recognized by authorship of those publications that report them.

Short publications usually present a simple idea that can be credited to one person—he who wrote the paper. Such papers usually have single authorship. Thus these rarely cause difficulty.

For major publications, however, we would suggest considering whether junior authorship should be used to recognize major scholarly or scientific contributions without which the study would have been much less valuable. For example, a statistical consultant might be recognized if the study design or method of analysis he suggested was new or unique and if this was largely responsible for the unusually illuminating study results. But obviously the statistician should not be a coauthor on every paper that reports on studies he helped design.

Contributions of scientific colleagues and supervisors are sometimes appropriately recognized by junior authorship. An example might be the creative role that some major professors play in suggesting and supervising graduate student research. Sometimes they are responsible for the ideas behind the study objective, the procedures, and the analysis. But not all major professors, colleagues, and supervisors make such contributions, and authorship should recognize contribution, not association.

Other kinds of contributions should be evaluated and perhaps recognized in this manner. We suggest the following be considered in deciding whether to add junior authors: the significance of the research findings and of the current report; the significance of the individual's scientific contribution; and perhaps whether his contribution will be recognized by authorship in a subsequent related publication.

If the problem analysis and project plan indicate that a multi-disciplinary or team approach would be best for a study, then it would be unfortunate if authorship considerations were allowed to discourage this approach. Nevertheless, our conventions about senior authorship and about scientific stature in relation to authorship do sometimes work disadvantageously in this way. For example, some researchers avoid teamwork because it may mean having their name third or fourth in a list of authors. Some readers may interpret this sharing of authorship to mean that the junior author's contribution may have been slight. And in conventional forms of literature citation, Dr. Smith of the Brown, Jones, and Smith team will be hidden "Brown *et al.*" Even an authors' note stating that all contributions are equal, and hence that authors' names are alphabetically arranged, does not remedy this difficulty.

Assignment of authorship, then, is both complex and important. The best general guide is that professional ethics and responsibility to co-authors and the scientific community come uppermost.

OBTAINING REVIEWS

When an author is finally satisfied with his manuscript, he is ready to have it reviewed. The practice of soliciting comments and suggestions from fellow scientists should not be considered mere ritual but, rather, an essential step in developing a manuscript. No author can be completely objective about his own work, nor can he have perfect insight concerning its ramifications. No matter how thorough a job he has done, his work can always benefit from a critical evaluation by his peers. So it behooves the author to take the business of reviewing seriously, to seek out good reviewers, and to duly consider what they have to say.

Manuscript reviews have a twofold purpose: to check the validity of the inferences and interpretations and to evaluate the adequacy of its presentation. Sometimes a single reviewer can perform both functions, but more often at least three or four are required: one or more technical reviewers, a statistical reviewer, an editorial reviewer, and perhaps a general reviewer. The technical reviewers should be specialists in the field or fields treated in the manuscript. The statistical and editorial reviewers should, if at all possible, be professionals trained in statistics and editing. The general reviewer can be of most help if he is a typical representative of the author's intended audience.

More and more research organizations are formalizing their manuscript review system. Many of them employ their own statisticians and editors and have a set procedure to assure adequate technical reviews internally. This is all to the good, of course, but it does not preclude getting independent reviews. In many instances, the most qualified reviewer is an "outsider," someone who is not only a leading expert in the author's field but who also may view things a little differently than members of the author's own organization.

Good reviewers are not easy to find. Besides having the background of experience appropriate to the subject at hand, a good reviewer must be willing to devote enough time and effort to the manuscript to be able to offer specific, constructive suggestions. If your immediate colleagues can't recommend some good reviewers, the only way to find them is by trial and error. As you send more and more manuscripts out for review you will begin to develop a list of preferred reviewers, those you know you can depend on to do a competent job. Avoid the "friendly" reviewer, the fellow who never has anything more to offer than "good contribution" or something just as innocuous. This kind of "review" may be good for your ego, but it doesn't help you improve your manuscript.

Because asking a fellow scientist to review your manuscript is really quite an imposition, courtesy demands you make his job as easy as possible. Send him a clean, legible, complete copy of the manuscript and tell him where you intend to publish it. Most important, specify exactly what you would like him to do. Do you want just a general review, or do you want him to concentrate on some particular phase of the manuscript—the statistical analysis, the conclusions and recommendations, or something else? Do you want him to stick to an evaluation of what you said and not worry about how you said it? Tell him, so he will not waste his time looking for split infinitives. Is there a particular point about the manuscript that bothers you? Clue him in. The more specific you can be, the more helpful he will be.

Receiving and using reviews is a skill you will develop with effort and maturity. It doesn't come naturally.

When you receive a particularly tough review, don't accept it as a personal affront. Remember, you asked for it. You evidently had enough respect for this person to request his help. So you owe it to him and to yourself to consider each of his questions and comments carefully and impersonally. You don't have to accept every suggestion, but if something bothered him enough to make a point of it, chances are it will bother someone else too. Maybe you can't accept his suggested revision, but you are at least alerted to a potential trouble spot and realize that some revision is probably in order.

Don't be impatient if he misunderstood you in some places. Remember, as author you are reading between and even behind the lines, so everything is clear to you. But the reviewer approached your manuscript cold—all he had to go on were the words before him. The reviewer is your trial audience—through his efforts you have one more chance to clean up the manuscript before exposing it to a wider audience. He has a more objective viewpoint.

When you have made the appropriate revisions inspired by his review and realize that the manuscript is better for it, write and tell him so. A brief word of thanks is all the reward he wants and by taking time to express your appreciation you have all but guaranteed his help on future manuscripts. Do not give in to the urge to "straighten him out" where he misunderstood or missed the point. Simply thank him for his comments and let it go at that.

PROVIDING REVIEWS

By receiving reviews from others you will find that some are helpful and some are not; some are easy to take, and some are not. Thus, you will discover that giving helpful reviews to others is a skill. And as a productive scientist it is a skill you will wish to develop. This task is hard work, it takes time, and it provides few personal rewards—but it is the professional responsibility of every member of the scientific community.

As a good general reviewer you are likely to put your scientific associate's manuscript to the same tests you use when you write your own. In one way or another, you will want to ask yourself these questions as you peruse his manuscript:

TITLE
    1.   Is it clear and definitive?
    2.   Is it too long?

INTRODUCTION
    1.   Does it justify the publication?
    2.   Does it clearly state the purpose?
    3.   Does it tell the reader what to expect in the balance of the publication?

PROCEDURES
    1.   Does it describe clearly and completely what was done?
    2.   Does it give all the information necessary for interpreting the results?

3. Does it give all the information necessary for evaluating the results?
4. Does it include irrelevant detail or information that could better be presented elsewhere?

RESULTS AND CONCLUSIONS
1. Does the author state clearly what he found?
2. Does he tell you what it means?
3. Are his conclusions and recommendations based on the results?
4. Does he distinguish clearly between conclusions and inferences?
5. Are his conclusions and recommendations reasonable?

SUMMARY OR ABSTRACT
1. Does it tell briefly what was done?
2. Does it tell what was found?
3. Does it state well the "big idea"?

TABLES
1. Are they well conceived and clear?
2. Do they help the reader to better understand the manuscript?
3. Are they all necessary?

PHOTOGRAPHS
1. Are the photos clear and in sharp focus?
2. Does each one illustrate the intended point?
3. Are any safety rules being violated in them?
4. Are any poor land-management practices shown unintentionally?

MAPS, CHARTS, AND GRAPHS
1. Are they presented in the best possible way?
2. Are they readily understandable?
3. Do they really improve the manuscript?

GENERAL
1. Is the writing clear, simple, and direct?
2. Is its tone suited to the intended audience?
3. Does the paper have unity and coherence?

4.   Do any parts appear to be unnecessary?
5.   Does the author's one "big idea" dominate?

IS THE PAPER WORTH PUBLISHING?

As a competent reviewer, you should be considerate; couch your criticism in the forms of questions or suggestions. Never be dogmatic or sarcastic. If you think the manuscript is too long, suggest ways to shorten it. If you don't like something, propose an alternative. Be specific in your comments—you cannot be vague and helpful at the same time.

THE SCIENTIST

Because we have attempted to define rather precisely a logical framework for research, some readers may infer that the recommended procedures will necessarily yield fruitful research. Unfortunately, this is not true. The fruitfulness of research depends mostly on the human aspects—the motivation and capability of the scientist himself. We believe this book provides information and views that will indeed help many researchers to be more fruitful, but unfortunately we have little new to offer on the scientist as a person.

You are not alone when you find yourself with important and profound questions about the role of science and scientists in society, about ways of improving the institutional environment for research, about how scientific creativity arises and can be nurtured. Both beginning researchers and experienced scientists continue to be interested in these questions. You will find stimulating views on these issues regularly expressed in such learned journals as *Science, American Scientist*, and *Daedalus*. Casual browsing among the titles on history and philosophy of science will show a wide range of books on these aspects of research.

We suggest you continue your scholarly reading in some of these areas. For a collection of papers and extensive bibliography about psychology of scientific creativity, the relations between the scientist's environment and his productivity, matching research problems and organizational environments with research people, and so on, we recommend *Scientific Creativity: Its Recognition and Development*, ed. Taylor and Barron (1963). Much less formal and widely read approaches to "the intellectual adventure of scientific research" are Beveridge's (1957), *The Art of Scientific Investigation*, and Platt's (1962), *The Excitement of Science*.

Reading on the relations of science, philosophy, and life, would be incomplete without reference to Whitehead's (1925) classic *Science and the Modern World*. Kemeny (1959) gives carefully written views on how a philosopher sees science, and the scientist's ability to conceptualize abstractions. Karl Pearson's (1892) *The Grammar of Science* and Popper's (1959) *The Logic of Scientific Discovery* are widely read treatises of the philosophy and methodologies of science.

Little Science, Big Science (Price 1963) deals with some of the ethical and organizational difficulties with the modern "research establishment." *The Double Helix* deals with the rivalries and other human frailties of scientists (Watson 1968). The general role of science in human endeavor is addressed by several writers in *Science and Culture*.[1] The promise and limitations of science and technology are carefully examined in modern context in Churchman's (1968) *Challenge to Reason*.

From these readings a young research scientist can gain a firmer understanding of what a scientific reputation is and how it is obtained; he will gain ideas about appropriate conduct in relation to colleagues on the same team and outside it. Unfortunately, none of these writings will give a realistic sketch of what a researcher may expect in his first job in research. That depends so much on the personalities of both researchers and research organizations that it seems impossible to offer useful general counsel. Suffice to say that scholarly autonomy will usually be earned with esteem, and for this some environments and reward systems are much better than others.

REFERENCES

BAKER, C. 1955. Technical publications, their purpose, preparation, and production. Wiley, New York. 302p.

BEVERIDGE, W.I.B. 1957. The art of scientific investigation, rev. ed. Random House, N.Y. 239p.

CHURCHMAN, C. W. 1968. Challenge to reason. McGraw-Hill, New York. 223p.

[1] This is the Winter, 1965, volume (vol. 94, no. 1) of Daedalus, J. Am., Acad. Arts and Sci.

EDITOR OF SCIENCE. 1965. Referees: anonymity and other problems. In Letters to the Editor. Science 150:1407-1408.

KEMENY, J. G. 1959. A philosopher looks at science. Van Nostrand, Princeton, N. J. 273p.

KREBS, H. A. 1968. The making of a scientist. Agric. Sci. Rev. 6(2):16-22. [also in Nature 215 (5107)].

PEARSON, K. 1892. The grammar of science. Walter Scott, London. 493p.

PLATT, J. R. 1962. The excitement of science. Houghton Mifflin, Boston 174p.

POPPER, K. R. 1959. The logic of scientific discovery. Hutchinson, London. 480p.

PRICE, D. J. 1963. Little science, big science. Columbia Univ. Press, New York 119p.

SHAW, B. T. 1967. The use of quality and quantity of publication as criteria for evaluating scientists. U.S.D.A. Misc. Publ. 1041. 78p.

STANDEN, A. 1950. Science is a sacred cow. E. P. Dutton, New York 221p.

TAYLOR, C.W., and F. BARRON, eds. 1963. Scientific creativity: its recognition and development. Wiley, New York. 419p. (Science Editions paperback, 1966)

WATSON, J. D. 1968. The double helix. Atheneum, New York.

WHITEHEAD, A.N. 1925. Science and the modern world. New American Library, N.Y. 191p.

12

AN EXHIBIT
OF RESEARCH PLANS

Many persons find that looking at actual research plans helps them gain more insight into the planning process. Reproduced here are two research plans—one a project plan, the other a plan for a component study—developed in general accord with the principles of problem-oriented research planning. They are not model plans, however. Skim them quickly to see how the various aspects of project and study planning, discussed in earlier chapters, come together in a research plan. Use these plans also to develop your critical faculties. By identifying some of their particular weaknesses, you will achieve a better grasp of research planning in general.

A PROJECT PLAN

The project plan shown below was developed at a U.S. Forest Service experiment station in 1960. Its subject matter is timber management and protection of an important species. It grew out of a long-term interest in this species on the part of station scientists and thus was built on a substantial fund of both ongoing and completed research. Research at Forest Service experiment stations, then as now, is organized by scientific discipline. The division of forest economics research initiated this project plan but it required the cooperation of other research divisions, outside research organizations, and action agencies as well. It proved to be a means of integrating a good deal of diverse scientific interest toward the solution to an explicit practical problem. This project was planned to employ about 12 man-years of effort during a 5-year period. Actually, more time than this has been needed, and the project still (1970) continues. Six major publications and a number of minor ones so far have resulted. More importantly, the research has produced significant modifications in both the actual management and protection of this timber species.

4800-2-2   March, 1960

WHITE PINE OPPORTUNITIES

PROJECT PLAN FOR
AN ECONOMIC ANALYSIS OF SEVERAL PEST-CONTROL AND MANAGEMENT ALTERNATIVES IN THE EAST

Robert J. Marty
Division of Forest Economics Research
Northeastern Forest Experiment Station
Forest Service, U.S.D.A.

TABLE OF CONTENTS

THE ECONOMICS OF WHITE PINE PRODUCTION IN THE EAST

PROJECT PLAN

1. THE PROBLEM

Forest Service Regions Seven and Eight contain more than 7 million acres of commercial forest land on which white pine is a major stand component. A great many persons own a part of this resource, many others are concerned with its management, still others depend on it as a basis for business operations or as a source of employment. The importance of the resource is apparent. What is not apparent, however, is whether this resource is contributing as it should be to individual prosperity and public welfare. Can the white pine resource be better managed?

1.1 HOW, AND HOW MUCH TO PRODUCE?

From an economic point of view, white pine management has two basic aspects. First we are concerned with the problem of *how to produce* white pine. We want to discover and use the most efficient methods of production, for this will mean that the greatest amount of white pine will be produced with the available land, labor, and capital. Or, looking at it another way, it will mean that the nation's white pine requirements will be met with the least possible expenditure of these resources, thus freeing the remainder for other productive uses.

There are three commonly employed methods of increasing pine production beyond the minimum available from the resource. We can increase the pine acreage, we can undertake management and protection activities in existing pine stands, and we can delay harvest to some extent beyond the age when the stand first becomes merchantable. Each of these ways of increasing production is, however, accompanied by a cost. In the first case we must invest additional land, labor, materials, and equipment. The second method calls for more labor, materials, and equipment, but no additional land. And to undertake the third alternative, we must be willing to wait longer for returns. It is the relative efficiency of these methods which is examined when we consider how to produce.

In determining the efficiency of management programs, we must be able to predict the biological result of each management program with reasonable accuracy. Then we must also predict what these results mean in dollars and cents. The most efficient programs are those which will yield the greatest amount of pine value per dollar of management costs.

The second problem is that of determining *how much to produce*. Our key to deciding how much to produce is this: It would be desirable for individual owners to expand production as long as the value of the additional pine more than compensated them for all the additional cost involved (including allowances for differences in risk and profit foregone on other available investments, assuming all other investments are at the margin). Up to this point, investment in additional pine results in more profit than could be obtained from other investments; beyond this point, resources could perhaps be better employed in producing other forest products.

1.2 WHO DOES THE PRODUCING?

Many different individuals acting independently make decisions of how and how much to produce. An understanding of the white pine problem must include an awareness of these individuals. Management decisions are made at two levels—by two separate groups. First, there are the private owners and public managers who are concerned with managing particular acreages of white pine. These decision-makers determine how, and how much white pine will be produced in the areas over which their management responsibilities extend. (Even when no conscious management practices are undertaken, the owner has made a decision. He has decided to accept the output that nature gives him.)

These managers differ in several important ways. They may have different sorts of white pine stands; they may differ in the amount of money they can afford to devote to white pine production; some may be interested only in returns which will accrue in the near future and others in returns over some longer span of time; they may have different opportunities for investing funds outside their white pine stands; they may be able to undertake management activities for widely differing costs; and they may anticipate widely differing prices for white pine. Thus, the most profitable method and amount of white pine production may readily differ for each of these individuals. From their standpoint the problems of how and how much to produce are influenced by their own unique circumstances.

The second major group of decision-makers includes the federal, state, and local governmental agencies which represent the public at large. These agencies cooperate in undertaking broad public programs designed to aid individual decision-makers in choosing the most efficient method and level of production (*e.g.* the C.F.M. program), in sharing the costs of production (*e.g.*, A.C.P., Soil Bank, and forest yield-tax laws), and in undertaking management activities which individuals could not efficiently undertake separately (*e.g.*, fire protection, pest control, and public tree nurseries). These programs indicate recognition that individual management efforts may not insure the most efficient production of the amount of white pine needed by the economy as a whole.

1.3 THE PROBLEM IS ONE OF ALLOCATING RESOURCES IN THE MOST PROFITABLE MANNER

By developing better information on the efficiency of various white pine management programs and criteria for choosing among these, we can be in a better position to help individual managers decide how and how much to produce. More efficient individual forest management is generally desirable from the social standpoint. In addition, such information can form the basis for better informed decisions on the appropriateness of public investment in specific white pine management activities. Such information would thus help to channel available private and public funds to their most productive uses. The problem, then, is one of developing information that will aid private managers and public agencies in allocating resources in such a way that the white pine resource contributes as much as possible to private prosperity and public welfare, and in fostering the dissemination and use of this information.

2. SCOPE

This project in the economics of white pine production is undertaken to examine some important aspects of the general problem outlined above. The purpose of the project is to place in the hands of decision-makers new information and decision techniques which will aid them in choosing efficient methods and appropriate levels of white pine production. The scope and limits of the project are discussed in this section. Its purpose is to make clear the scientific aspects of the general problem which will be included in the project.

2.1   MANAGERS AND PEST-CONTROL AGENCIES ARE TREATED SEPARATELY

Two groups of decision-makers will be considered, and treated separately:

1.   Government agencies with white pine pest-control responsibilities in R-7 and R-8.
2.   Private and public decision-makers with white pine management responsibilities in the Northeast.

Managers of white pine stands must choose among a number of cultural operations, protection activities, and harvest dates in formulating a management program. Pest-control agencies, on the other hand, consider only the advisability of instituting blister-rust and weevil control. The decisions of these two groups differ because a different set of management activities is available to each.

Then, too, the value of pest control is measured in part by the value to the economy of additional stumpage. This is often greater than value to the private owner.[1]

Also, managers frequently determine how and how much to produce simultaneously, whereas pest-control agencies first allocate currently available funds in the most efficient manner and then make judgments on optimum program size for future years.

The decision-making environments of these two groups serve to orient the analysis. These groups include most of the firms, agencies,

[1] As in all economic analyses it will be possible to estimate only the costs and returns to pest control and management that can be objectively measured in dollar terms. Thus, any change in volume, size, and quality of stumpage that will influence timber values will be taken into consideration. The influence of pest control and management on aesthetic and other currently nonmeasurable values must be ignored on this level. Thus, it is evident that an economic analysis does not provide final solutions. What it does provide is an objective evaluation of the profitability of various alternatives as far as profitability can be judged on the basis of measurable costs and returns. By quantifying this much of the problem, the necessary judgment decisions can be more explicitly stated and thus more easily made.

and individuals who are directly concerned with white pine timber production. By assessing management opportunities and limitations for these two groups, the project will provide a better basis for assessing the need for other forms of public action in white pine production.

2.2 SOME MIXED STANDS ARE CONSIDERED

Some white pine volume is harvested from stands containing only scattered white pine trees. These stands are managed primarily for other species. Management recommendations based on the white pine component of mixed stands will have an unknown influence on other stand components. For instance, release of scattered white pine will also influence the growth and yield of surrounding hardwoods. Mixed stand management recommendations thus require knowledge about biotic and economic factors affecting all stand components— knowledge that is not currently available.

The management analysis will be designed to apply to those stands that will be managed to develop a pure pine stand. In other words, the analysis will assume that the manager has already decided to devote his stand exclusively to white pine production. This means that other stand components will be considered only inasmuch as they influence the growth and yield of pine.

If the stand under consideration is currently (*i.e.*, at the time of analysis) pure white pine, then this restriction raises no problems. And it should be noted that even in areas that are usually considered mixed pine-hardwood types, pine stands can often be delineated in such a way that they contain essentially pure pine.

In cases where this is not possible because of a rather intimate intermixture of hardwoods, the situation may differ. If the hardwood species present in the stand are expected to have no market during the rotation, or if they have a low value relative to pine, then the analysis procedure will still be essentially correct because it assumes no value for nonpine components.

In stands where salable hardwoods are intimately intermixed with pine, the analysis procedure will introduce a management bias because the value of these salable hardwoods will be ignored. The greater the amount of salable hardwoods present relative to pine, the greater this bias will be. It is evident that the analysis procedure should not be applied to stands of this sort.

This may not be as serious a limitation of the analysis method as it first appears, however, because areas supporting salable hardwoods, especially those with values comparable to white pine, are not typically thought of as pine sites at all. It would indeed be useful to include mixed-stand management among the management alternatives, but the current lack of knowledge about mixed-stand growth-response, yields, and values, prevents their inclusion.

The pest-control analysis procedure will include all stands that contain white pine, because pine pest-control activities have less influence on the other stand components.

2.3 SIX MANAGEMENT AND PEST-CONTROL ACTIVITIES ARE ANALYZED

The management and pest-control activities considered in the analyses include thinning to concentrate growth on crop trees, release cutting to control stand composition and improve pine growth, pruning to improve quality, weevil and blister-rust control to reduce loss from forest pests, and selection of a time of harvest to control the stand condition at harvest.

Further investment of capital and labor on the current acreage of white pine makes for more intensive management. An alternate method of increasing the output of white pine is to plant or encourage natural regeneration. Currently, however, young white pine stands can be purchased for less than it costs to establish new stands in many areas in the East. This evidence indicates that the most promising investment opportunities involve some form of further management intensification as compared with expanding the acreage of pine. For this reason, regeneration is not included among the management activities.

3. OBJECTIVES

The basic purpose of this project is to obtain information that will aid both private and public decision-makers in evaluating their opportunities in eastern white pine timber production. Specifically, it will:

1. Provide private and public forest managers with criteria for selecting the most profitable management program for their white pine stands.
2. Provide forest-pest-control agencies with criteria for evaluating the profitability of various activities for controlling pests of white pine in individual stands.

3. Provide forest-pest-control agencies with criteria for allocating pest-control funds most efficiently among white pine stands.
4. Estimate the prospective supply of white pine in the East, 1960-2000, under various assumptions of management, cut, and pest-control intensity.
5. Analyze alternate distributions and levels of white pine pest-control activities in the East, 1965-1975.

4. PLAN OF WORK

This project will require the joint efforts of specialists in Forest Research and the Division of State and Private Forestry. This section outlines the information needed to meet the objectives indicated in Section 3. When the best available knowledge and experience appears inadequate additional studies are proposed and briefly outlined. The plan of work includes the following sections:

4.1 Prediction of gross yield for stands of differing initial character, future management, and time of harvest.
4.2 Prediction of the reduction in gross yield due to insects, disease, and other causes.
4.3 Preduction of the yield-saving associated with blister-rust and weevil control.
4.4 Estimation of the future value of white pine stumpage.
4.5 Estimation of the cost of management and pest-control activities.
4.6 Formulation of management and pest-control guides for individual stands.
4.7 Determination of the current nature and extent of the white pine resource in the East.
4.8 Formulation of pest-control fund-allocation criteria, future white pine supply projections, and guides to desirable pest-control program scope.

4.1 GROSS YIELD IS DETERMINED BY RATE OF GROWTH AND TIME OF HARVEST

To estimate the efficiency of various management and pest-control programs, it is first necessary to determine the anticipated gross yield at harvest for stands having different biological characteristics and under various levels of management. Gross yield at harvest is a function of initial stand condition, future management, and number of years to harvest (Fig. 1).

4.11 Initial Stand Condition and Future Management Define Rate of Growth

Three measures of development together provide a basis for evaluating the value growth of a white pine stand: dbh growth, board-foot volume growth, and quality-index increment. These in turn are determined by initial stand condition and future management.

Measures of initial stand condition include site quality and stocking. Site quality is a measure of the growth potential of the forest site. An adequate measure of stocking involves the following factors: percentage of stand area occupied by white pine; the density of pine in stocked areas; pine size, vigor, and quality; and the type and amount of competing vegetation.

Growth of pure, even-aged pine. We will first determine average dbh and volume growth in essentially pure, even-aged pine stands. The Division of Forest Management Research, NEFES, is currently conducting a study of the growth of white pine in the Northeast. This study involves periodic remeasurement of both sample trees and plots in the major white pine producing areas of New England. Data on periodic growth from the first remeasurement of these plots and trees will be used to correlate dbh and volume growth rates with initial stand condition in pure stands.

Dbh growth of pure even-aged pine = f (site quality, initial average tree size and vigor, and pine density and distribution).

Volume growth of pure even-aged pine = g (site quality, initial average tree size and vigor, and pine density and distribution).

These relationships will provide an estimate of dbh and volume growth for any initial stand condition likely to be encountered in pure, even-aged northeastern white pine stands. These relationships will be extended in two important ways. First, we will be able to determine growth rates through many years of stand development. For instance, if at the end of the remeasurement period sample stand A looks about like sample stand B did at the beginning of the period, we will assume that stand A will exhibit stand B's growth rate during the next remeasurement period. By connecting growth rates of various

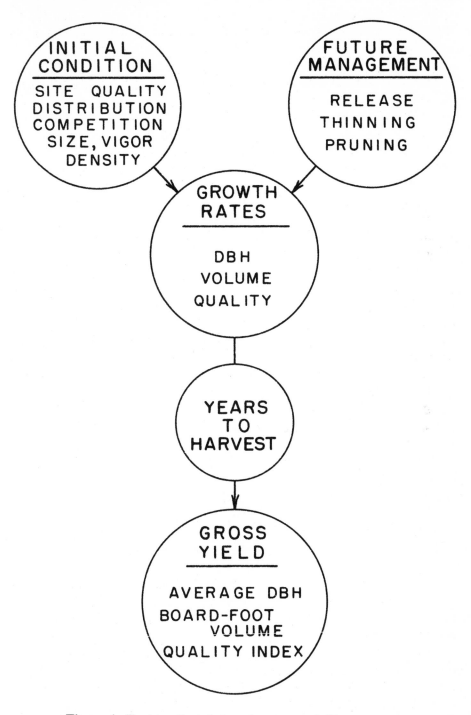

Figure 1. Factors that determine gross yield of a stand.

sample stands in this manner, we will obtain growth profiles extending over many years for stands of differing initial character.

The second extension of these relationships will be a determination of the effect of thinning on growth rates. For instance, if sample stand A were thinned so as to look like sample stand C, then we presumably would have altered stand A's growth rates to those of stand C. We can, therefore, specify thinning regimes which will maximize growth rate or meet any other criteria we propose. Thus, we will introduce the influence of the first management activity at this point in the analysis.

These growth estimates will be compared with other available data on white pine growth and yield[2] and the extrapolations necessary to cover southeastern conditions.

Growth of overtopped pine. Rates of growth are, however, further conditioned by the presence of competing vegetation, particularly in the form of an overstory. A special study will be undertaken to establish the effect of overstory on growth rates in stands overtopped by species and amounts of vegetation which will cause negligible mortality but significant growth reduction. Interest in the effect of overtopping is restricted to the less severe overstory conditions, because experience indicates that heavy overstory competition of the type provided by maple, beech, and certain oaks makes it most difficult (unprofitable) to maintain the pine component. In these circumstances it is not anticipated that the essentially pure pine objective assumed here will be economically desirable.

[2] Other major sources of data include:

1. HUSCH and LYFORD. 1956. White pine growth and soil relationships in southeastern New Hampshire. Bull. 95. Agri. Exp. Sta., Univ. New Hampshire.

2. SMITHERS, L. A. 1954. Thinning in red and white pine stands at Petawawa Forest Experiment Station. Canada Forestry Br. Silvic Res. Note 105.

3. FROTHINGHAM, E. M. 1914. White pine under forest management. U.S.D.A. Bull. 13.

4. GEVORKIANTZ, S. R., and ZON, Raphael. Second growth white pine in Wisconsin. Wis. Agri. Exp. Sta. Bull. 98.

5. FOREST SURVEY. 1958. South Maine Growth Study Plan NEFES Unpub.

6. VEMMERSTEDT, John. 1959. White pine yield SEFES Unpub.

Study 1. *The influence of Overstory on White Pine Growth Rates and Terminal Injury Rates*

Problem: How much is dbh and volume growth reduced by the presence of overstory competition in white pine?

Scope: Data to be collected in the East. Several overstory classes to be sampled.

Objective: Quantify the relationship between dbh and volume growth rate and overstory class stratified by the other initial stand conditions, and the relationship between overstory class and terminal injury rate.

Methods: Several classes of overstory involving species and degree of crown density will be delineated which show significant differences in degree of competition afforded. Harvard Forest records of overstory effect will be classified as to initial stand condition and overstory characteristics. Missing data will be developed by measuring 5-year periodic dbh and height growth in other white pine stands. Data will be analyzed on a sample tree basis by regression techniques. These growth rates will then be compared with normal (nonovertopped) growth rates to estimate reduction in normal growth rates. Observations will at the same time be made of the rate and severity of leader injury and these will be correlated with overstory condition.

This study will be designed to quantify the following relationships:

Dbh growth of overtopped pine = h (site quality, initial tree size and vigor and overstory class).

Volume growth of overtopped pine = i (site quality, initial tree size and vigor, and overstory class).

As these relationships will be based on data of limited extent, we will use them as a correction factor for the pure, even-aged growth relationship.

Reduction in normal dbh growth due to overtopping = j (pure, even-aged growth and overtopped volume growth).

Reduction in normal volume growth due to overtopping = k (pure, even-aged growth and overtopped volume growth).

These last two relationships will allow us to estimate the effect of a second management activity—release. We can expect growth rates to increase in the amounts indicated by these last two relationships if pine is released from the competitive overstory.

Quality increment. The effect of initial stand condition and future management on quality increment is the final relationship to be established.

White pine log grading research carried on at NEFES indicated that there appears to be little difference in quality index (QI) at harvest among unpruned white pine stands of ages 50 to 100 which have been subject to the same degree of weevil injury. Increases in QI depend on the presence of a significant volume of logs free of coarse knots and weevil injury. Therefore, a single average QI will be used for all unpruned stands subject to the same level of weevil injury.

The effect of pruning on QI at harvest will also be included in the analysis. The basis for this estimate will be a theoretical study already completed in connection with the Lake States white pine study[3]. Theoretical information must be employed, because there are too few pruned white pine stands of merchantable size to provide a basis for empirical testing. Factors considered include QI without pruning, size of trees at pruning, size of trees at harvest, and height of pruning. This information will provide an estimate of the increase in QI associated with pruning of different intensities, undertaken in stands of various present sizes, and for various times of harvest.[4]

QI increase from pruning = 1 (QI without pruning, tree size at pruning, height of pruning, proportion of trees pruned, and tree size at harvest.).

The seven relationships, f through l, define the rate of gross growth that will be anticipated from stands of differing initial stand condition and future management.

Gross yield at harvest is then determined by these growth rates and anticipated number of years to harvest.

4.2 EXPECTED LOSS FROM INSECTS, DISEASES, AND OTHER CAUSES WILL BE DEDUCTED FROM GROSS YIELD.

These estimates of gross yield must be refined by considering the anticipated losses due to insects, diseases, and other destructive agents (Fig. 2). This section describes the studies needed to predict the magnitude of losses to insects and diseases without pest control. The modifying influence of control effort is considered in Section 4.3.

The ability to predict loss varies among destructive agents. Enough information is available for the two primary pests of white

[3]AMIDON, E. L., and Marty, R. J. 1957. Office report on pruning eastern white pine. NEFES.
[4]The effect of weevil injury rate and weevil control on QI is considered in Sections 4.2 and 4.3.

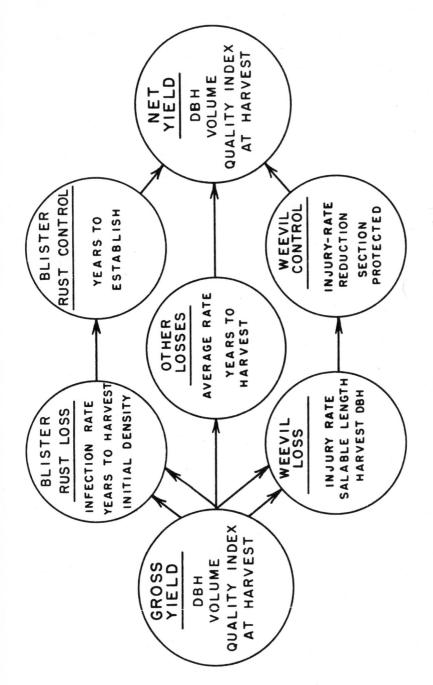

Figure 2. Procedure for estimating net yield of white pine from gross yield and the factors that influence losses from insects and diseases.

pine, blister rust and white pine weevil, to attempt a comparatively refined estimation of loss on a stand or small-area basis. Losses from other causes are generally erratic in occurrence and of less importance. More general estimates of expected loss will be employed for these.

4.21 *The rate of fatal infection indicates blister-rust loss.*

Yield will be reduced by blister-rust infection in many white pine stands. To estimate the amount of loss we will estimate the rate of infection and the relationship between infection rate and yield loss. Forest pathologists indicate that little significant reduction in growth occurs during the incipient stages of pine infection. The problem then becomes one of predicting the rate of *fatal* infection—the average annual rate of infection that will eventually cause tree mortality.

The following factors seem important in determining the annual rate of fatal infection. First, the spore-producing capacity of the species of ribes in the area. This is a function of the susceptibility of the particular species of ribes and the ribes leaf surface present within and around the stand. Second, the air moisture and temperature during the spread of sporidia is important. Temperature must be below 70 degrees F. and free moisture must be present for approximately 12 hours before sporidia can infect pine.

Sporidia production takes place in the late summer and early fall and temperature and humidity conditions are probably responsible for the commonly observed phenomenon of an infection-rate reduction from north to south over broad geographic areas, as well as the marked changes in infection rate associated with aspect and elevational differences within small areas. Third, relative crown size and dead length of pine are probably important factors within the stand. Relative crown size determines the "target size" of a pine in relation to other stand individuals, with the largest crowns offering a larger than average target and thus an increased probability of infection. Dead length determines the distance from sporidia-producing centers, with the assumption that infected ribes are evenly distributed throughout the stand.

A recent study of rust infection rates in the Lake States[5] revealed that infection rate varied primarily by geographic location. Within geographic hazard zones, infection rate did not vary significantly with ribes population. Apparently any ribes population above a very low

[5]King, D.E. 1958. Incidence of white pine blister rust infection in the Lake States. LSFES, Sta. Paper 64.

level had equivalent ability to infect pine. Also no significant variation in infection rate was observed among trees of different target size (as measured by dbh) within hazard zones. A special study (Study 2) will be initiated in the East to establish rates of fatal infection, using as a guide the information contained in previous infection-rate surveys carried out in the East.

Study 2. *Blister rust infection rates in the East*

Problem: What are the rates of fatal blister-rust infection in the eastern states?

Scope: The full range of blister-rust infection conditions in the East.

Objective: To establish average annual rate of fatal infection for stands differing in species and population of ribes, tree size distribution, and rust hazard.

Methods: Eastern states white pine stands in which ribes eradication has recently been undertaken will be stratified by geographic location, and a random sample drawn within each stratum. Blister-rust control records will establish the ribes population at time of control. Hazard conditions will be estimated by control personnel acquainted with each area. Number of trees fatally infected by diameter class will be determined on transects within each sample area. Data will be analyzed by regression techniques to establish average infection rates and to test for significant differences in infection rate among geographic locations, ribes population sizes, hazard conditions, pine d.b.h. classes, dead length, and crown class.

This study will indicate the relationship between the rate of fatal infection and standard hazard conditions.

Average Rate of Fatal B. R. Infection = m (Species of ribes, ribes population, rust hazard, geographic location, dbh class, dead-length class, and crown class.).

A second aspect of blister-rust loss is the relationship between infection rate and yield loss. If, as in the Lake States, infection occurs essentially at random among individuals of any stand (does not vary significantly with dbh, crown, or dead-length class within stands), then we can assume that mortality from blister rust may influence either harvest volume, or average dbh at harvest, or both, but have no predictable effect on quality. The average rate of fatal infection will be assumed constant over the life of a stand and will be expressible as a percentage mortality per year randomly distributed among stand individuals

The relationship between injury rate and yield loss involves several factors. The first of these is the number of years to harvest, which will determine the proportion of stand individuals that will be unmerchantable by harvest. For instance, a stand within 20 years of harvest may not experience any loss from future blister-rust infection because it often takes this long for an infection to kill the tree. On the other hand, a stand 50 years from harvest may lose 30 percent of its present stocking by future infection if the rate of infection is like that experienced in the Lake States' high-hazard zone.

Second, initial density also plays a part. Blister-rust infection can be pictured as a random thinning. Such a thinning may not be serious in a stand with heavy initial stocking. An equal proportion of mortality in lightly stocked stands, however, may seriously reduce harvest volume and change average dbh at harvest.

Change in harvest volume and dbh due to blister-rust infection = n (Initial stand condition, number of years to harvest, and infection rate.)

Study 2 will provide the basis for predicting the loss to be anticipated from uncontrolled blister-rust infection. Establishment of anticipated infection rates and the distribution of infection among stand individuals will allow direct prediction of the yield of losses associated with this pest by application of expected mortality to gross-yield information (Section 4.1).

4.22 *White pine weevil injury causes both volume and quality loss.*

Foresters have long been aware of the extensive damage caused by the white pine weevil in eastern white pine stands. Weevil injury results in two major types of loss. First, destruction of the terminal leader results in forking, crook, sweep, and increased taper, which cause a reduction in recoverable volume. Second, weevil injury causes lumber degrade in the remaining volume. To determine the magnitude of volume and quality loss to be anticipated in white pine stands, an estimate of the future rate of weevil injury is needed, and the relationship between injury rate and yield loss must be established.

If approximately the same rate of injury can be anticipated throughout the merchantable length, then a usable estimate of future injury rate is contained in the number of injuries that have already occurred in a particular stand. Three separate studies indicate that the rate of weevil injury does not vary markedly with height, above the first 4-8 feet.[6] Provisionally, this method of prediction will be employed in the analysis procedure.

The relationship between injury rate and volume loss has recently been examined[7]. This study was conducted in southeastern New Hampshire, where a sample of 300 white pine of merchantable size was taken in twelve undisturbed white pine stands. Volume loss was hypothesized to be determined by (1) the number of injuries the tree has sustained, (2) the position of injuries in the bole, (3) the deviation from normal form associated with each injury, and (4) the tree's age and inherent growth pattern.

Volume loss was estimated by subtracting observed tree volume from the volume of an unweeviled tree of equal total height and dbh. Volume loss was correlated with dbh and a weevil injury summation (number of injuries weighted by height).

Volume loss due to weevil injury = p (rate of weevil injury, number of trees at harvest, average harvest dbh, and merchantable height.).

As a part of this project, additional areas will be sampled to extend the geographic range of the study, and refinements in the methods of variable measurement will be introduced (Study 3). In addition, an attempt will be made to determine the average proportion of all leader injuries caused by *Pissodes strobi*. This relationship will provide the basis for predicting the volume loss associated with weevil injury.

The relationship between injury rate and quality loss has also been recently studied[8]. In connection with a white pine log-grade

[6]1. OSTRANDER, M. D. 1957. Weevil Attacks Apparently Unrelated to Height of Eastern White Pine. NEFES Res. Note 67.

2. MARTY, R. J. 1959. Predicting weevil-caused volume loss in white pine. Forest Sci. 5:3.

3. WILSON, R. 1959. White pine growth study plot data, NEFES. Unpub.

[7]MARTY, R. J. *Loc. cit.*

[8]OSTRANDER, M. D., and STOLTENBERG, C. H. 1957. Value loss from weevil-caused defects in eastern white pine lumber. NEFES. Res. Note 73.

study carried out at the Pack Forest, Warrensburg, New York, a tally was made of the grade yield of lumber produced from 400 logs, many of which were weeviled. Records were kept of the amount of degrade resulting from weevil-caused defects such as cross grain, large branch knots, red rot, and reaction wood. Estimates were made of the dollar value of degrade per log by number of weevil injuries.

As a part of this project, data from other locations will be collected and degrade will be expressed as a QI loss per M.B.F. (Study 4). The resulting relationship will be used to predict the QI loss associated with various rates of weevil injury.

Quality loss due to weevil injuries = q (rate of weevil injury.).

These two studies together will allow prediction of the volume and quality loss to be expected in various white pine stands that are subject to different rates of weevil injury.

4.23 Yield loss from other causes will be included in a general risk factor.

Probable losses from other causes must also be estimated. These include loss from fire, other insects and diseases, weather, and animals. Because there appears to be no acceptable basis for predicting the magnitude of these losses on an individual stand basis, they will be included in a general risk factor that will be applied to all stands.

In considering any particular stand, many of these causes of loss are erratic in occurrence. Average losses over large geographic areas, however, can be estimated. Such average loss figures are of use in planning activities covering broad areas, because investment is spread over enough stands so that the average loss is, in fact, likely to be experienced. Estimates of the magnitude of average losses due to fire, weather, and animals will be derived from estimates contained in Forest Resources Report No. 14[9]. Forest entomologists indicate that yield losses due to insects other than white pine weevil are on the order of 1 percent during short rotations. As a basis for predicting nonblister-rust disease losses, White's work in Canada will be used[10].

[9]FOREST SERVICE USDA. 1958. Timber resources for America's future. Forest Resource Report No. 14.

[10]WHITE, L. T. 1953. Studies in forest pathology-decay in white pine in the Timogami Lake and Ottawa Valley areas. Canadian J. Bot. 31:175-200.

If there appears to be a significant variation in the magnitude of loss by geographic area, different risk factors will be used for each state or group of states.

To the individual manager, such a risk rate must be interpreted differently. He faces not a 5 percent volume loss caused by these factors, but a 5 percent probability of catastrophic loss involving the majority of stand volume. This is particularly true in the case of fire and wind damage. Therefore, this risk factor contains an essentially different meaning for those concerned with management of limited forest acreages.

4.3 THE REDUCTION IN LOSS ASSOCIATED WITH PEST CONTROL IS A FUNCTION OF REDUCTION IN INJURY RATE OR INFECTION RATE.

The saving in yield at harvest associated with pest control is directly predictable from the relationships outlined in Sections 4.1 and 4.2, if the impact of control on infection rate is predictable.

4.31 Blister-rust control implies complete protection.

If Lake States' experience is indicative of blister-rust relationships in the East, no reduction in rate of infection is afforded by partial eradication of *ribes*. In this case, only one level of eradication can be logically considered—practically complete eradication.

Complete eradication of *ribes* does not imply, however, that the total yield loss associated with blister rust will be prevented, even when past losses are ignored. In most instances, several years are required to attain complete eradication—years during which the rate of fatal infection continues essentially unchecked. Thus the proportion of future loss that can be prevented is affected by the number of years needed to establish complete control.

The time required to establish control is, in turn, determined by the number of workings necessary and the average number of years between workings. Both will be estimated by blister-rust control personnel for individual control blocks. Number of workings depends on the climatic, edaphic, and *ribes* stocking conditions in individual control blocks. These conditions control the time necessary for ribes to reappear after working and thus the number of years between workings.

If control can be established after a single working and it is undertaken soon after appraisal, virtually all future loss can be prevented. If, on the other hand, control cannot be attained until the stand is within twenty years of harvest, almost none of the yield loss will be prevented. Schedules will be prepared to show the proportion of potential future loss from blister rust that can be prevented by various combinations of number of years to harvest, number of workings, years between workings, and rust infection rate.

4.32 Partial protection is often advisable in weevil control.

In contrast to rust control, partial control of weevils is effective and frequently desirable. Insecticides can be applied at various times during the life of the stand, and it may thus be possible to influence the attack rate during any particular period of height growth. If attack rate can be influenced, the rate of injury can be controlled, to some extent at least, in any selected portion of the bole that will develop in the future. For instance, in a stand currently 10 feet in average total height, any portion of the bole above 10 feet may be subject to protection.

It is logical to initiate control as soon as possible and to favor young stands, because the volume loss associated with injury is directly proportional to the volume of the injured log at harvest. This means that injury becomes steadily less important as the trees become taller, because a lower-volume and lower-value portion of the bole is affected. There is, then, a relationship of this form: every additional foot of bole protected results in less yield saved than the previous foot.

4.4 STUMPAGE PRICE ESTIMATION INCLUDES THREE STEPS

White pine stumpage is converted primarily into lumber. Therefore, the value of stumpage to the usual buyer is determined by the price of lumber and the buyer's costs of converting stumpage into lumber (which includes a profit margin). Evidently the maximum stumpage price that a processor would be willing to pay is given by the lumber value contained in a stand less all the costs of its conversion. This maximum stumpage price will be termed "stumpage value."

Stumpage value is an appropriate value estimate to employ in determining the return to cooperative pest control. This is so because the nation always receives the entire stumpage value regardless of how it is distributed between the stumpage producer and the processor.

From the stumpage producer's standpoint, however, stumpage value may not be a good estimate of the price he can expect. This is frequently true because differences in stand quality go unrecognized and because the seller is in a less advantageous market position vis-a-vis the processor. Thus, the stumpage grower may be more interested in stumpage "price" than he is in "value."

Stumpage value estimates thus depend on two other projections: future lumber price for various grades of white pine lumber, and the future costs of conversion for various types of white pine stands. To estimate stumpage price a third projection is needed—the proportion of future stumpage value that will be reflected in stumpage price.

4.41 A lumber price projection is already available.

A projection of white pine lumber price for the current average grade mix was developed and employed in the Lake States' white pine study[11]. This projection will form the basis for lumber price projection in this project as well. The projection indicates an annual increase in lumber price relative to other commodities on the order of 0.5 percent of the base price over the projection period (1958-2010). Factors considered in this projection include past lumber price trends and changes in costs of production, in demand for wood products, and in the cost and supply of competing materials.

4.42 Conversion-cost estimates will include all costs.

The lumber value represented by any white pine stand can now be estimated. Lumber value is determined by the stand's volume and grade yield distribution at harvest, and the lumber price estimates for that date. To estimate stumpage value, the cost of conversion must be subtracted from lumber value.

Cost of conversion here includes costs of logging and milling white pine and an overhead and profit margin. We are interested in estimating the average total cost of converting stumpage to lumber ready for sale at the mill. Overhead and profit are included in costs because these costs, too, must be covered in the long run. No operator would be willing to continue production for long if he could not meet overhead expenses and make a normal profit on his operation.

[11]KING, D. B., C. H. STOLTENBERG, and R. J. MARTY.
1960. The economics of white pine blister rust control in the Lake States. In process.

Unit costs of logging and milling vary with such factors as the logging or milling techniques and equipment, stand volume per acre and tree size distribution, the stand's lumber grade mix, the nature of the logging chance, and the cost of labor and equipment operation. A study now being planned at NEFES will provide estimates of these relationships[12]. With these data, it will be possible to determine how current logging and milling costs vary for stands of different types and for different sorts of logging and milling operations.

The problem of estimating overhead expenses and profit margins representative of an industry is difficult on both theoretical and practical grounds. The approach used here will be to estimate a representative ratio of gross profit (before taxes) to sales for the industry as an estimate of required profit margin. Overhead expenses consist mainly of depreciation charges. An estimate of depreciation charges can be made that considers current equipment and plant value, equipment life, and replacement costs.[13]

All these cost elements will be projected to future years by considering changes that are likely to occur in logging and milling methods, and in the cost of labor and equipment. It will then be possible to estimate the total average cost of conversion for stands of different types. The residual of lumber value less conversion cost will indicate anticipated stumpage value at harvest.

4.43 The proportion of stumpage value reflected in price depends on local market conditions.

The proportion of stumpage value that the stumpage producer can expect in the future will depend primarily on two factors. First, how much competition exists among lumber producers for available stumpage. And second, how well informed and advised stumpage producers are about market conditions, methods of sale, and the volume and quality of their stands.

These factors, and thus stumpage price, vary markedly from area to area and can be expected to change with time as well. In general, both buyer competition and seller knowledge can be expected to

[12] A study of factors affecting white pine tree harvesting and milling costs. Plan being prepared by Barney Dowdle.

[13] The problem of estimating profit margin and depreciation allowance is well illustrated by: WEINTRAUB and SIDNEY. 1958. An examination of some economic aspects of forest service stumpage prices and appraisal policies. Forest Service, inc.

increase in future years, which indicates a general rise in the proportion of stumpage value reflected in stumpage prices.

The current ratios of stumpage value to price, and the degree to which they will change in various white pine market areas are both unknown, however. These ratios are not amenable to objective prediction with the present level of knowledge in forest economics.

Therefore, three future stumpage value-price ratios will be proposed and employed in the management analysis. These ratios will be designed to include the range of ratios most likely to actually exist in future years in white pine markets in the east. The choice of a ratio most nearly approximating the price expectations in particular market areas or for particular managers will thus be provided and left to those applying the analysis, who are presumably in the best position to judge expectations in their own circumstances.

4.5 THE VALUE OF MANAGEMENT AND PEST CONTROL MUST BE COMPARED WITH THEIR COST.

The first four sections of this Project Plan have shown the various elements that determine the dollar value of the additional yield associated with various management and pest control activities. A cost is associated with each of these activities as well, however, and an estimate of this cost is required to judge the profitability of any activity or set of activities.

Like value, cost is made up of two major elements: physical cost as measured in man and machine hours and required items such as materials; and the dollar value of these physical inputs. It is useful to separate the two, because, although physical costs remain relatively stable both from year to year and from area to area, their dollar value may vary considerably.

4.51 Pest-control costs are readily available.

Blister rust can currently be controlled in several ways. The *ribes* population can be eliminated by hand or chemical means, and it now appears that the rust may also be controlled by treating the pine itself with systemic chemicals.

Cooperative Forest Pest Control has employed both hand and chemical methods of eliminating *ribes*, and considerable control experience has been accumulated for both. Control cost for these methods is a function of the *ribes* population (size, number, and distribution of plants) at time of control, and the rate of *ribes* regeneration after initial control. For any particular stand, control personnel are able to estimate (1) the number of man-days of labor necessary to complete the initial working, and (2) the total number of workings that will be required to control blister-rust infection in the stand.

By determining the relationship of number of man-days necessary for the first working and that necessary for successive workings, and the average number of years between workings, an estimate can be derived of the total man-days of control effort necessary for the stand, and their distribution in time. We will rely on Cooperative Forest Pest Control for estimates of these factors from their control experience in the East.

Cooperative Forest Pest-Control records will be used to determine the current average dollar cost per man-day for both chemical and hand control. These average costs will include all operating expenses, which include reconnaissance, supervision, and overhead. The trend in this dollar cost will be determined for a series of past years and the indicated trend projected to the future, based on anticipated changes in labor and material costs.

The potential availability of a method of salvaging already fatally infected pine with systemics (*e.g.* acti-dione) introduces the possibility of saving stocking that would otherwise be lost regardless of the application of the older control methods. This additional protective measure might best be applied where there is enough fatally infected stocking to cause a reduction in yield at harvest, the value of which exceeds the cost of protection. To determine the cost of this measure for a particular stand, an estimate is needed of the number of trees per acre that will require treatment to insure the maximum yield at harvest. This estimate multiplied by the cost of treatment per tree will give average cost per acre. This additional method of control will be included in the analysis if data become available as to its effectiveness and cost within study time limits.

White pine weevil control can currently be obtained by two methods: chemical control from the ground using hand spraying equipment, and chemical control from the air. The ground method of control involves spraying of all or a selected portion of the white pine in the spring or fall with any of several insecticides. This is a practical method of control for stands less than ten feet in average height at time of treatment. Physical cost data for this method are available from research carried out at NEFES[14].

[14]CROSBY, David. 1958. Control of white pine weevil with insecticidal emulsions. NEFES Res. Note 78.

Aerial application of insecticides is currently the only feasible method of protecting stands more than ten feet in average height and may be less expensive for control programs covering large areas. Pilot tests of this method of control in New York State have shown that the helicopter is the most efficient aircraft type, and have tested the effectiveness of various insecticides and carriers. The average number of aircraft hours required per acre (including loading and waiting time), the amount of insecticide needed per acre, and the man-hours of reconnaissance and supervision required will be estimated from the experience in the New York State pilot tests.

4.52 Only the variable costs of management are of interest.

The costs of management considered here include the costs of thinning, release and improvement cutting, and pruning. There are, of course, other costs of management such as land taxes, administrative expenses, and inventory and sales costs. These costs do not depend on the management program undertaken; they are stable for any single owner. Therefore, they are not part of the cost that is required to undertake these additional management activities. We are concerned only with the increase in cost, which is to be compared with the increase in return associated with these management activities. The management analysis thus assumes that the owner has already decided to hold his pine land and to devote it to white pine production. The remaining problem faced by such an owner is the choice among several white pine management programs.

Thinning, release, and improvement cuttings all remove certain stand individuals from the competitive complex. As concerns cost, these operations are analogous. When these operations yield merchantable material they become, essentially, logging operations. The physical cost of logging various types and amounts of material will be available from the study of logging costs mentioned in Section 4.42. The removal of nonmerchantable material may be accomplished by silvicides as well as by logging. Physical cost data for various types of silvicidal treatment will be taken from the many studies already reported[15]. The cost data on logging and chemical control will be used to estimate where each is least costly in achieving the desired result. In this way, it will be possible to determine the least-cost method of carrying out any particular thinning, improvement cutting, or release operation. Methods requiring equipment not generally available to forest-land owners will not be considered.

[15] For instance, a bibliography of some 80 articles is in: RUDOLF, P.O., and R.F. WATT. 1956. Chemical control of brush and trees in the Lake States. LSFES Sta. Paper 41. Selected references are also at the NEFES.

The cost of the remaining cultural operation, pruning, depends on such factors as number of trees pruned per acre, average number of whorls in the pruned section, average number of limbs per whorl, average limb size, and the pruning method chosen. Estimates of how physical factors vary with stand condition are available from a Harvard Forest study[16]. Another study carried out in Michigan indicates how pruning time per limb varies under different pruning methods[17]. These data will be used to determine the cost of pruning under various stand conditions and for various intensities of pruning.

After estimates of the physical cost of these operations have been obtained from the indicated sources, they will be compared with the experience of service and consulting foresters. Estimates will then be adjusted where they appear to differ significantly from actual experience in white pine regions in the East.

Finally, the physical cost data will be translated to dollar terms under several assumptions of labor and equipment cost that reflect the range in these dollar costs expected to be encountered in the future. No single estimate of costs will be chosen from these, because it is likely that dollar costs will vary considerably from owner to owner. Rather, the cost estimate applicable to a particular owner will be chosen from a set of possible costs when the analysis of his management opportunities is made.

4.6 PEST-CONTROL AND MANAGEMENT GUIDES FOR INDIVIDUAL STANDS WILL AID CFPC AND MANAGERS IN CHOOSING PROFITABLE INVESTMENTS.

The biological and economic data so far described in the plan of work will be used to formulate management and pest-control guides for individual stands. The purpose of these guides is to aid pest-control personnel in choosing the most efficient type and level of pest control for particular stands; and to aid professional foresters in recommending the most profitable program of management for particular stands. In this section we will outline (1) the information needed to estimate the profitability of pest control or management alternatives, (2) the way in which the data so far developed are to be

[16]Tarvox, E. E., and P. M. Reed. 1924. Quality and Growth of White Pine is influenced by Density, Site, and Associated Species. Harvard Forest Bull. 7.

[17]RALSTON, R. A., and W. LEMMIEN. 1956. Pruning pine plantations in Michigan. Mich. Agr. Exp. Sta. Cir. Bull. 221

organized to provide this information, and (3) how profitability information provides a system within which choices can readily be made (Fig. 3).

4.61 Both guides require a knowledge of stand conditions and what investments others will undertake.

Both CFPC and individual managers need an estimate of the profitability of the alternate pest-control or management activities open to them in particular white pine stands. The value of pest control in a particular stand depends on (1) the initial stand condition and the seriousness of pests and other causes of loss, and (2) the future management (including number of years to harvest) that the manager will choose for the stand. The pest control guide thus calls for preliminary estimates of stand and pest conditions and future management.

To determine the profitability of alternate management programs we must again be aware of the stand and pest conditions, but in this case, we must estimate the pest control that will be undertaken in the future. With this information we will be able to determine the profitability of the various management programs applicable to the stand.

4.62 Yield data will be reduced to a number of discrete classes.

Net yield without additional pest control or management is determined by the stand and pest conditions, and the number of years to harvest. A table will be prepared to show the net yield anticipated from several different stand and pest condition classes, and number of years to harvest. The table will be formulated so that significant, and approximately equal, differences in yield exist between condition classes. Contemplated, then, is a reduction of the continuous yield function to a manageable set of discrete condition classes with corresponding yields. This yield table will foster recognition of significant differences in stand and pest conditions, and will reduce the subjectivity of yield estimation by explicitly recognizing more of the factors that influence yield than have been usual in American yield tables.

In considering either pest control or management, we are again faced with a large number of possible programs. Not only are there several different pest control activities, for instance, but at least some of these can be applied at various levels. The changes in yield associated with each pest control or management activity will be based

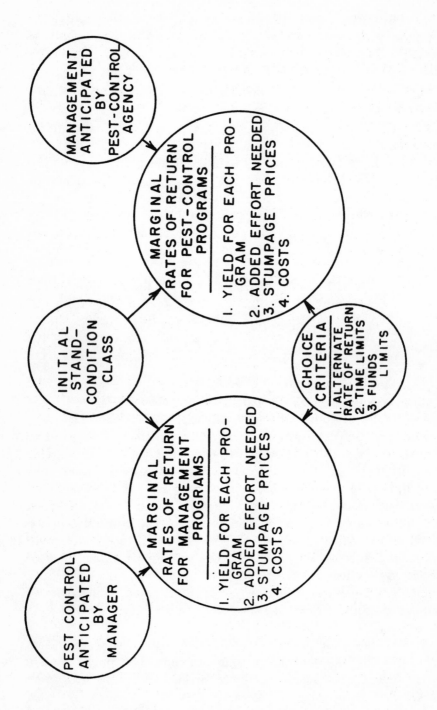

Figure 3. Factors that determine the most profitable program of management or pest control.

on the optimum (most profitable) level for the activity. By considering only optimum levels we can reduce the number of pest-control or management programs to a reasonable number of alternatives not inconsistent with profit maximization.

Finally, our interest will focus on the additional yield from marginal increments of pest control or management investment. We must know not only how profitable a particular pest control program is likely to be, but what profit is associated with increasing the intensity of pest control from, for instance, blister-rust control alone to blister-rust and weevil control.

4.63 Choices among programs are based on marginal economic analysis.

We will determine the value of the marginal yield from each of the possible pest-control or management programs. We will also have available estimates of the additional cost of undertaking each of these programs. Upon knowing the cost and return associated with each program we can express its profitability in terms of the interest rate that equates these costs and returns. Such an interest rate can be calculated for each pest-control program under consideration for the stand.

We will also determine the best order in which to consider additional pest-control or management activities in any particular stand. As additional activities are considered total program cost increases, and this additional investment is accompanied by a decreasing marginal rate of return, because we are always proceeding to less profitable activities.

In general, both CFPC and managers choose among the programs open to them by undertaking additional activities until the marginal rate of return available on the next activity is less than that wthat could be earned by investing elsewhere. The greatest rate of return available on investment outside the stand thus determines the most profitable pest-control or management intensity. This alternate rate of return is a function of available funds and the total spectrum of available investment opportunities. Private managers frequently have some idea of the rate of return they can expect from nonforest investments. The appropriate alternate rate to employ in CFPC decisions will require special study (see Section 4.81).

The manager may be prevented from undertaking the most profitable management program for at least two reasons. First, the funds he has available for management may not be sufficient to allow him to reach the most profitable intensity of management; and second, the most profitable program may require a harvest date not acceptable to him. We can take these funds and time limitations into account by restricting consideration to those programs within the manager's reach both in terms of total cost and rotation age[18]. The process of profit maximization remains the same within this reduced set of alternatives.

Note that the economic analysis planned here will (1) be based on estimates of growth, yield, costs, and prices that may be incorrect for particular stands and owners, and (2) exclude many nonmonetary factors such as the influence of changes in pine management program on the recreational, water, and aesthetic values of the stand. We cannot expect, therefore, that owners will always feel that the apparently "most-profitable" program is indeed the most desirable when consideration is given to (1) the desire to reduce the risk of loss on marginal changes in management programs and (2) the influence of management on factors not included in the analysis. The analysis, however, will provide very useful information for making these judgment decisions. For instance, an owner may choose a "sub-optimal" management program because he feels the risk associated with the "optimal" program is too great, or because it adversely affects other values he desires from his stand. In such a case, the analysis will provide the owner with an estimate of the dollar return he must forego to secure less risk or insure nonmeasurable benefits. This information will make such judgment decisions more explicit and thus more easily and correctly made. The same reasoning applies to the pest-control analysis.

4.7 AN ESTIMATE OF WHITE PINE RESOURCE IN THE EAST IS NEEDED TO JUDGE FUTURE SUPPLY AND PEST CONTROL PROGRAM SIZE.

To determine the supply of white pine likely to be forthcoming in future years and the level of cooperative pest control that will be

---

[18]Although managers frequently have a firm idea of the amount of funds they are willing to devote to forest management, they may not be aware of whether they will be able to maintain investment in forest stands much beyond the age when stands first become merchantable. The ability to delay harvest so as to maximize profits may be closely correlated with ownership characteristics such as asset size and structure. A study designed to correlate time of harvest with ownership characteristics of this sort might provide a better basis for recognizing owners who have potential time limitations.

most advantageous, it will be necessary to ascertain the current extent and condition of the resource.

White pine stands will be sampled to obtain estimates of their condition class. By establishing these classes, inferences can be drawn directly from the individual guides on stand management and pest control as to the most likely yield under different assumptions on management and pest control.

To estimate the proportion of total white pine acreage in the East that lies in each of the stand classes, a stratified random sample of pine acreage will be undertaken.

Study 5. *White Pine Stand Condition Class Survey*

Problem: What is the extent and condition of the present white pine resource in the East?

Scope: A random sample of all white pine stands mapped by CFPC in Regions 7 and 8.

Objective: To determine the proportion of total acreage in the East in each of the condition classes.

Methods: The total white pine acreage in the East will be stratified by state and by three size classes (reproduction, poletimber, and sawtimber). Stands to be sampled will be drawn at random from within strata. Sample stands will be subsampled to determine the average condition class for each sample stand.

The universe that is of interest is the entire acreage of white pine in Regions 7 and 8. Samples will be drawn only from that proportion of total acreage so far incorporated in CFPC records. Survey results will be applied to acreages not included in the survey if this will give unbiased results (where excluded acreages do not differ significantly from the distribution of condition classes within the sampled area). Where bias would result from this procedure, additional "spot" surveys may have to be undertaken if these acreages are large.

4.8 FUTURE SUPPLY ESTIMATES ARE NEEDED BY GOVERNMENT, INDUSTRY, AND PRODUCERS.

The condition class survey, coupled with the management and pest-control guides, allows the examination of several interesting aspects of the white pine resource from an overall standpoint.

4.81 The condition class survey allows the formulation of guides for optimum allocation of pest-control funds.

First, we are able to show a method of allocating available pest-control funds among stands in the East. The condition class survey will yield an estimate of the number of acres in each condition class. Cooperative Forest Pest Control might, then, well assume some average level of management over all condition classes[19]. These two factors (condition class plus management) would determine the profitability of the various pest-control programs for each class. A table could then be prepared in which the various condition-class pest-control-program combinations were arranged in descending order according to marginal rate of return. A corresponding list of cumulative control cost would accompany this listing. By going down the list until cumulative cost equaled prospectively available funds, the marginal (lowest acceptable) rate of return would be indicated. This rate of return would provide an approximate guide in determining the most profitable pest control program for individual stands.

This guide might be used as follows: First, several stand classes might not yield acceptable rates of return on any pest-control program. These could immediately be excluded from consideration for pest-control investment if there were no special reasons for including them. Second, the analysis made for individual stands under consideration for pest control would yield a listing of rates of return as indicated in Section 4.63. The appropriate program would be that one whose marginal rate of return most nearly equaled the marginal rate determined by considering all stands. In this way the final choice criterion for individual stands is provided. In general by allocating in this way, available funds will be invested in a manner that will maximize the benefits from pest control.

4.82 Future supplies will be estimated

An additional use of the condition-class survey is to estimate the total supply of white pine forthcoming under various assumptions of management. We will prepare estimates of what prospective white pine stumpage inventories would be under these specific assumptions:

1. Pest control and management at the present level.

2. Pest control at the present level and management at the most likely future level.

3. Pest control at the present level and management at a social-optimum level (ignoring funds and time limits).

[19]Some of these condition classes will be a type to which the management guides will not apply. The pine yields from these classes will be assumed to remain unchanged.

The first estimate will indicate the minimum supply that can be expected in the future. The second will indicate the most likely supply to be forthcoming in the future under the assumption that pest-control activity continues at the present level. And the last estimate would indicate the potential supply that could be generated if pest control remained at the present level and other management activities were intensified to an optimum level.

Another set of estimates will involve the most likely management level in the future, together with several alternate levels of pest control. This would indicate how much supply could be increased by altering pest-control investment in the future and provide a guide to the amount of future pest-control investment that might be judged as most desirable.

In addition to providing information of use to the Cooperative Forest Pest Control in planning future programs, supply information will be of interest to public agencies in judging whether additional incentives to more intensive management would be desirable and to industry in judging whether adjustments in harvesting, processing, and marketing activities would be necessary under new supply conditions.

5. PRESENTATION OF RESULTS

This project includes many phases that are of interest primarily to rather select audiences. Therefore we expect to publish the results of this project in a number of separate papers, each dealing with those aspects of the study that are of interest to specific groups.

Outlined below are several of the expected publications, with content, authorship, publication media, and audience indicated.

(1) White Pine Pest-Control Opportunities in the East.

This paper will take the form of an "in service" report to Cooperative Forest Pest Control that briefly summarizes the project methods and presents the major project results of interest to CFPC.

1. The current distribution of white pine stands in the East by condition class, pest hazard, etc.

2. An explanation of optimum procedure for allocating white pine pest-control funds.

3. Estimates of the distribution of profitable control sites under various assumptions of future management, price levels, etc.

4. Analysis of alternate levels and distributions of white pine pest-control activity for 1965-1975.

This report will be authored by FER, NE.

(2) Pest Control Guides for White Pine.

This paper should be a CFPC field manual that explains in detail the application of the pest-control analysis procedure to individual stands. It will be accompanied by work tools to simplify field application. The manual will be aimed at the Control Aid level and assume introduction by organized training sessions. Authorship should be shared by Pest Control, R-7 and R-8, and FER, NE.

(3) The White Pine Management Guide.

This publication will be written for the professional forester who manages or advises on the management of white pine. It will explain the application of the management analysis procedure to individual stands in much the same form as in Paper 2. It will also be accompanied by work tools to simplify field application. Authorship of this station paper will rest with FER and FMR, NE. If a separate guide is needed in the Southern Appalachians, FER, NE will provide the Southeastern Station with the relevant data available from this study.

(4) The Prospective Supply of White Pine in the East.

This paper will present the estimate of white pine supply by 2000 under the assumption of the most likely level of management and pest control. It will be aimed at industry and white pine landowners. FER, NE will author this publication and it will appear in an appropriate lumber trade journal.

(5) Blister-Rust Infection in the East.

This report will summarize the results of Study 2 of this project and will appear as a station paper authored by FER or FDR, NE.

(6) The Influence of Weevil Damage on White Pine Yield.

This paper will appear as a station paper and summarize the results of the two studies of the influence of weevil injury on the volume and quality of white pine. It will be authored by FER, NE.

6. SCHEDULE AND ASSIGNMENTS

Successful completion of this project will require using the talents and knowledge of specialists in many fields of forest administration and research. Indeed, many of these have already been used in the preparation of this work plan. However, primary responsibility for planning and carrying out particular phases of the project logically rests with a somewhat smaller group.

This section of the plan indicates the unit that will have primary responsibility for each phase of the project. Others may be called upon to help plan, conduct, or prepare reports on individual studies, but they are not included in this outline unless they have major responsibilities.

A tentative schedule is also indicated. The major factor limiting completion of the project is White Pine Growth Study. A sufficient number of plots must be established and then remeasured before the factors affecting growth can quantitatively be evaluated. Three-year remeasurements from approximately 75 plots will be available in late 1962. We believe this number will be sufficient to meet the needs of this study.

Task	Primary agency	Completion date	Man-months
1. Project plan	FER-NE	March 1960	6
2. White pine growth study	FMR-NE	Jan. 1963	36
3. Effect of overstory on growth & leader injury (Study 1)			
Work plan	FMR-NE	June 1961	1
Conduct & analysis	FMR-NE	Oct. 1961	5
4. Effect of thinning & pruning	FER-NE	July 1963	1
5. Rust incidence survey (Study 2)			
Work plan	FER-NE	Sept. 1960	1
Conduct	R-7, 8	May 1961	15
Analysis & publication	FER-NE	July 1961	2
6. Weevil-volume loss (Study 3)			
Work plan	FER-NE	July 1960	1
Conduct	FER-NE	Sept. 1960	2
Analysis & publication	FER-NE	Oct. 1960	1
7. Weevil-quality loss (Study 4)			
Work plan	FER-NE	July 1960	1
Conduct	FER-NE	Dec. 1960	2
Analysis & publication	FER-NE	Jan. 1961	1
8. Yield table formulation	FER-NE	June 1963	5
9. Stumpage values & prices	FER-NE	July 1962	12

10. Pest control costs	R-7, 8 & FER-NE	July 1963	1
11. Management Costs	R-7, 8 & FER-NE	Feb. 1964	1
12. Pest control guides			
Analysis	FER-NE	Nov. 1963	10
Publication	FER-NE & R-7, 8	Jan 1964	2
13. Management guides			
Analysis	FER-NE	April 1964	10
Publication	FER-FMR-NE	June 1964	2
14. Condition class survey			
Work plan	FER-NE	Jan. 1962	1
Conduct	R-7, 8	March 1964	24
Analysis	FER-NE	July 1964	3
15. Current pest control opportunities	FER-NE	Dec. 1964	2
16. Future white pine supply outlook	FER-NE	Mar. 1965	2
17. Future pest control program scope	FER-NE	June 1965	2

Work-Load Summary

Unit	Man-Months
FER-NE	61
FMR-NE	43
R-7, 8	41

	145

A STUDY PLAN

The study plan "Volume Loss Due to Weevil Injury in Eastern White Pine," reproduced below, is the third of four studies outlined in the project plan. Its purpose was to establish the effect of weevil injury on timber yield under a variety of circumstances. So the study involved elements both of formulating and of testing a model, and specifying the model so that yield-loss predictions could be provided. As it turned out, this study was not entirely successful. The model proved to be too simple to account for much of the observed variation. Obviously, other sources of variation than those accounted for have a significant impact. This is not an unusual circumstance in research. Study of this phenomenon has not yet progressed far enough to provide highly accurate predictions. The estimator developed was used in the resulting publication[1] to provide estimates of volume loss, because it was the best then available. It is hoped someone will delve more deeply into this process and provide an improved predictive model.

4800-2-2 August 1960

VOLUME LOSS DUE TO WEEVIL INJURY IN EASTERN WHITE PINE

A STUDY PLAN

Robert J. Marty

Division of Forest Economics Research
Northeastern Forest Experiment Station
Forest Service, USDA

TABLE OF CONTENTS

[1] MARTY, R., and D. G. MOTT. 1964. Evaluating and scheduling white-pine weevil control in the northwest. U.S. For. Service Res. Paper NE-19. 56p. illus. p. 14-17.

FS-4-el-1.5

Robert J. Marty
August, 1960

VOLUME LOSS DUE TO WEEVIL INJURY IN EASTERN WHITE PINE

A WORK PLAN

THE PROBLEM

The Northeastern Forest Experiment Station, in cooperation with others, has recently undertaken a project assessing eastern white pine timber production opportunities for private owners and government agencies[1]. This work plan describes research that is part of that larger project. The purpose of the research planned here is to secure information that will allow us to predict the volume lost by weevil injury in eastern white pine stands.

To assess the importance of loss and of controlling white pine weevil attack, we need estimates of (1) the amount of weevil injury to be expected, (2) the resulting volume loss, (3) the added loss due to lumber degrade in the remaining volume, (4) the reduction in loss to be expected from control measures, (5) the cost of control, and (6) the future value of white pine lumber.

The research project in the economics of eastern white pine management and pest control will eventually provide information in all these categories. This work plan outlines methods for determining the information needed in the first two. We need better estimates of the amount of weevil injury to be expected in individual white pine stands, and the volume losses that various injury intensities will generate.

Expected Rates of Injury. Several recent investigations have shown that the rate of weevil injury varies with the height of white pine trees. And this variability follows a predictable pattern. Apparently it takes some time for weevil populations to build up to significant levels in young white pine stands. Injury rates typically increase gradually and culminate between 24 and 32 feet. Thereafter, the attack rate diminishes but apparently never disappears.

This injury pattern has been noted in most white pine stands examined. The actual rate of injury may, of course, vary from stand to

[1]MARTY, R. J. 1960. White pine opportunities—a project plan for economic analysis of several pest control and management alternatives in the east. NEFES, Forest Service, USDA Unpub.

stand. This variation in absolute rates of injury is probably related to environmental factors that influence the capacity of the area for supporting a weevil population.

The rather constant relative rates of injury at various heights in the tree suggest a useful approach in determining the amount of weevil injury to be anticipated during future years. Given the average number of injuries that have already occurred, and the current height of the stand, relative attack rates will allow a direct prediction of the number of injuries to be expected, on the average, during any subsequent period of stand development.

Volume Loss. The amount of volume loss associated with any particular attack depends on (1) the height of attack, which determines whether a high- or low-volume portion of the bole will be affected; (2) the severity of attack, which influences the initial deviation from normal form; (3) the tree's age at harvest, which determines the length of time available for subsequent recovery; and, (4) the tree's environment, which, together with the above, determines the form and amount of post-injury development.

The problem here is one of determining how the volume loss, resulting from weevil injury of average severity, is affected by height of attack, the length of post-injury development, and the tree's environment. Previous study has demonstrated that the average volume loss associated with a single injury declines as the height of injury increases. This follows from the fact that injuries high in the tree influence the volume of upper logs, which contain a small proportion of total volume.

Although this is the general tendency, much variation exists in the response of individual trees to weevil injury. Part of this variation may be ascribed to the site quality. But the average volume loss that will be evident over an entire stand is closely related to these factors.

PREVIOUS RESEARCH

Two recent studies dealing with volume loss in white pine from weevil injury have been published. In the first of these[2] the researchers have described the loss in cubic-foot and board-foot volume apparent in the present white pine stands in New Hampshire. Forest survey plots in white pine stands were revisited, and pole and sawtimber-size trees measured. In pole-size trees the authors found

[2] WATERS, W. E., T. MCINTYRE, and D. CROSBY. 1955. Loss in volume of white pine in New Hampshire caused by the white pine weevil. J. Forestry 53:271-274.

that loss in cubic-foot volume was related to reduction in merchantable height. In sawtimber-size trees, loss in board-foot volume was attributed to reduction in merchantable height, and to crook and other cull within merchantable length.

In this study no correlation was attempted between number of weevilings and volume loss. The results, therefore, represent the average volume loss attributable to weeviling in white pine stands now present in New Hampshire, over all sites and stand conditions and for all degrees of attack incidence.

Because many sawtimber-size trees are residual individuals left after logging, they represent trees of less than average merchantability largely from the excessive weeviling. Thus, these data were not intended to be used as a basis for prediction, but rather to provide a description of the present resource. And as such, they are extremely revealing with respect to the amount of volume loss that may occur if weevil injury is allowed to progress unchecked. These researchers found that volume loss among sawtimber-size trees averaged 40 percent of the sawlog volume anticipated if weevil injury had not occurred.

A second study[3] carried on in the same general area, had as its purpose the development of an equation that would allow prediction of the loss in board-foot volume in merchantable white pine caused by weevil injury. In this study some 300 white pine of merchantable size were examined, the current merchantable volume determined, the height and number of injuries noted, and an estimate made of normal volume (that is, the volume that would have been present if no weeviling had occurred). Volume loss (normal volume less observed volume) was related to the position and number of injuries noted. The resulting regression relationship provided a means of predicting volume loss.

A third as yet unpublished study,[4] carried out in New York, had a somewhat different purpose. In this study an attempt was made to relate the incidence of weevil injury to various environmental factors. The study attempts to develop guides for determining the absolute rate of injury to be expected under various environmental conditions. The researchers found a consistent correlation between injury rates and certain soil characteristics. As a part of this study, they also

[3]MARTY, R. J. 1959. Predicting weevil-caused volume loss in white pine. Forest Sci. 5:269-274.

[4]CONNALA, D. P., *et al.* 1960. White pine weevil injury in New York plantations. New York State Sci. Serv. Unpub.

investigated the relationship of injury rate to tree height. The same general relationship as noted above was found by these researchers in white pine plantations in New York.

OBJECTIVES
　　The objectives of this study are as follows:
　　(1) To extend the geographic area of the previous study of volume loss study, with certain modifications in observational procedure and analysis introduced.
　　(2) To quantify the relationship between tree height and relative number of injuries.
　　(3) To test the correlation between observed rates of injury in the lower portion of the bole and the rates of injury higher in the tree.

SCOPE
　　Volume loss will be determined in terms of board-feet, because this is the volume measure used in most sales of eastern white pine stands. Data will be collected in white pine stands located throughout the Northeast; namely, in the states of Maine, New Hampshire, Vermont, Massachusetts, Connecticut, Pennsylvania, and New York. This geographic coverage should insure applicability of study results wherever in the eastern states weevil injury is a serious problem in white pine management.

VOLUME LOSS
　　The original study. In the original study[5] volume-loss attributable to weeviling was determined for each tree as follows: The current merchantable board-foot volume of the tree was determined by estimating the length, scaling diameter, and cull percent for each merchantable log in the tree. A 1-foot stump was assumed, and a 6-inch top taken as a limit of merchantability unless large branches, sweep, or crook limited merchantable height below this point. The pulpwood volume contained in tops and large limbs was ignored. This board-foot volume was termed "the observed volume," and was an estimate of net board-foot volume contained in the tree at time of measurement.
　　The net board-foot volume the tree would have contained had it not been weeviled was then estimated. The diameter of the tree was assumed to be unaffected by weeviling. An estimate of the merchantable height had the tree been unweeviled was taken from

[5] MARTY, R. J. Op. cit., p5.

curves of merchantable height to a 6-inch top over dbh and total height based on measurements of unweeviled white pine. Form class if unweeviled was determined by measuring from 3 to 5 trees on each plot which had no apparent weevil-like injuries below 17.3 feet.

With these estimates of diameter, merchantable height, and form class, a volume determination was made by Bickford's form class volume tables[6]. Although this estimate of what net volume would have been without weeviling is obviously crude, results were encouraging. For the trees in our sample that seem to show little or no divergence from normal form had observed volumes that differed little from the calculated unweeviled volumes. Volume loss was determined by subtracting observed volume from "normal volume" for each tree in the sample.

Normal volume determines the amount of volume that could be affected by weevil injury. Thus, a single weevil attack of average severity might result in different volume losses on a tree of large volume as compared to one of small volume. Observed dbh was taken as an indicator of the amount of normal volume.

The location of each observed weevil-like injury was marked on a diagram of the tree prepared in the field. The effect of an injury on volume is largely restricted to the log within which it occurs, but sometimes extends to the logs above. Thus, an injury occurring within the first log has a larger potential effect than one occurring in any subsequent log, mainly because the volume of the butt log is larger. The number of injuries occurring within each 16 feet of merchantable length was determined, and these numbers were weighted by dividing them by the log number. The weighted number of injuries in each log was then summed over all logs in the tree.

This weighting assumes that a weevil attack occurring within the first 16 feet above the stump generates twice the volume loss of one occurring in the second 15-foot section, three times the loss of one in the third 15-foot section, etc. Attacks occurring above unweeviled merchantable height were ignored because they have no effect on the amount of volume loss. A regression analysis was then run on the data, which resulted in the following predictive equation:

Bd.-Ft. Loss = 2.08 (dbh-8 in.) (Weevil Injury Summation)   1

---

[6]BICKFORD, C. A. 1951. Form-class volume tables for estimating board-foot contents of northern conifers. NEFES Sta. Paper 3.

Reformulating the Hypothesis. Field data from this original study have been reexamined in an attempt to reformulate the hypothesis in a manner that more nearly reflects the variation in observed data.

First, a fundamental change in the dependent variable was needed. Volume loss, the original dependent variable, is given by normal volume less observed volume. And normal volume is at least implicit in dbh, part of the original independent variable. This formulation casts some doubt on dependence and independence of the two variables.

Instead of volume loss, observed volume is used as the dependent variable in the new hypothesis. Observed volume then becomes a function of normal volume and the amount of injury:

$$\text{Observed Volume} = b_1 \text{ (Normal Volume)} + b_2 \text{ (Amount of Injury)} \qquad 2$$

Second, we were unsatisfied with the weighting scheme adopted in the original summation of injury. Therefore, new weights are introduced. Instead of assuming that an injury in the second log always causes half the volume loss one in the first log, the new weighting scheme assumes that the importance of an injury is directly related to the percentage of total volume contained in the particular section within which the injury occurs.

The injury summation now indicates the average number of times each board foot in the tree has been subject to weevil injury. Thus, if 50 percent of normal volume were contained in the butt log of a 3-log tree and this log were weeviled twice, this is assumed to be equivalent to having each log om the tree weeviled once.

The new summation of injury is then multiplied by normal volume. The product of the weevil-injury summation and normal volume thus gives the equivalent number of board feet influenced by weevil injury, and is termed the weighted injury summation, WI. The hypothesis now becomes:

$$OV = b_1 \text{ (NV)} + b_2 \text{ (WI)} \qquad 3$$

and we expect that b_1 will be close to unity, and that b_2 will be negative and represent the average proportion that is lost of each board foot affected by a weevil injury.

Finally, we noted in statistical reexamination of the original data that variance is not homogeneous. Instead, variance seems to increase as the square of normal volume. Therefore to restore homogeneity, observations will be weighted by the inverse of the square of normal volume:

$$1/NV^2[OV = b_1 (NV) + b_2 (WI)]$$

4

RATE OF INJURY

The second objective is to quantify the relationship between tree height and the proportion of injuries. The number of injuries occurring in each 8-foot section will be determined for each tree in the sample.

Proportions may differ among trees in the sample for four reasons. First, of course, there will be random variation from one individual to the next that will be reflected in variance estimates. Second, taller trees will have different proportions than shorter ones because their total number of injuries is greater and spread over more sections of the bole. Third, differences may occur because of tree location. For instance, locality A may have had well-developed weevil population when sample trees became established, but in locality B the weevil population may have built up as a result of pine establishment. Fourth, it is not equally easy to distinguish past injury in pine of all sizes. The larger the diameter of the section of the bole within which injury occurred, the more probable it is that the injury will go unnoticed. This means that the sample observations may show lower proportions of injuries in the butt sections of large trees than will be observed in small trees.

In examining injury rates, attention will be restricted to injuries that have occurred within normal merchantable length, because these are the only injuries that influence board-foot volume. To test for the effect of inability to discern all injuries in the butt sections of large trees, the following test will be performed. The average proportion of injuries in each 8-foot section, and their variances, will be computed for all 2-log trees in the sample. And equivalent proportions and variances will be computed for all sample trees with normal merchantable lengths of 4 logs or more. These proportions will be based only on that which have been observed within the first four 8-foot sections.

Proportions pertaining to the same section in each tree group will then be paired and a test made to determine whether they differ significantly:

$P_{ij} = n_{ij}/N_j$, when 5

P_{ij} = proportion of injuries observed in the ith sections of the jth tree group.

n_{ij} = number of injuries in the ith sections of the jth group

N_j = total number of injuries observed in the jth group

The variance of each proportion is then given by:

$$V(P_{ij}) = P_{ij} (1-P_{ij}/N_j$$ 6

And the test for a significant difference among paired proportions takes the form:

$$(P_{11} - P_{12}) - t(V_{P_{11}} + V_{P_{12}})^{\frac{1}{2}}$$

$$< \pi_{11} - \pi_{12} < (P_{11} - P_{12}) + t(V_{P_{11}} + V_{P_{12}})^{\frac{1}{2}}$$ 7

If these tests show that proportions are significantly lower in the butt sections of large trees, then observations of numbers of injuries in butt sections of large trees will be corrected (increased) so that proportions in larger trees correspond with those found in small trees.

Tests of the sort proposed above will also be used to compare proportions among groups of trees from different stands to determine whether some significant difference of this sort exists. It is anticipated that such differences will not be marked.

Finally, corrected sample distributions for each merchantable height class will be prepared, along with estimates of the range within which the true distribution is likely to fall.

Next, simple regression analyses will be undertaken of the following form:

$y_i = bx_i$, when

y_i = the number of injuries observed in the ith section (s) of the tree, and

x_i = the number of injuries expected, based on the number of injuries that have occurred below and the average injury distribution for trees of the same merchantable height.

These analyses will result in variance statements that reflect the accuracy of predictions of future injury rates based on the rates that have already occurred.

SAMPLING PROCEDURE

Samples of white pine trees will be drawn in the following manner. A sample of 500 trees will be gathered in groups of 50. Two such 50-tree groups will be located in New York, two in New Hampshire, two in Maine: and one each in Pennsylvania, Connecticut, Massachusetts, and Vermont. The ten 50-tree groups will be chosen in such a way that a range of diameters is encountered. All groups will be made up of trees 9 inches or larger dbh, and will be located in stands that show no evidence of past cutting or natural disturbance.

The following data will be gathered for each 50-tree group.

(1) *Site index*. Site index will be determined by measuring the total height and age at dbh of at least three dominant, essentially unweeviled white pine within, or in the vicinity of, the 50-tree group. Height and age figures will be averaged over the three trees, 8 years added to age at dbh, and site index curves prepared in connection with the Lake States White Pine Study[7] used in the determination of site index.

For each sample tree the following information will be collected.

(1) *Current volume*. Current volume will be estimated ocularly assuming a 1-foot stump and a 6-inch d.i.b. merchantability limit, except where merchantability is limited by large branches, crook, or other factors.

(2) *The number and position of weevil-like injuries*. After trees have been scaled, the number of injuries that occur in each 8-foot section of the bole will be recorded. Injuries will not be recorded above normal merchantable length.

ANALYSIS

Field sampling will provide measurements of dbh and total height for each sample tree. Data from individual white pine tree studies provide estimates of the average form class and merchantable length for unweeviled pine of given total height and dbh. Thus, we can associate with each sample tree a normal dbh, merchantable length, and form class. And these will be used to determine normal volume by Bickford's form-class volume tables[8].

This procedure assumes that both dbh and total height are unaffected by weeviling. This is a reasonable assumption as far as dbh

---

[7] KING, D. B., C. H. STOLTENBERG, and R. J. MARTY. 1960. "The economics of white pine blister rust control in the Lake States." Forest Service, USDA.
[8] Bickford Op. Cit. p. 8.

is concerned. The total height assumption is more questionable. Analysis of preliminary data taken in the original study reveals no significant differences in height that could be associated with differences in weevil-injury rates. This evidence leads us to believe that where weevil injury is light-to-moderate no significant reduction in total height results from weeviling. Where weevil injury is severe, however, total height is definitely reduced. For sample trees where the total height-dbh relationship is obviously other than normal, tree age will be determined and combined with the site index to estimate normal total height.

With all primary variables now available, the analyses specified above can be carried out. Use, where practicable, will be made of automatic data processing equipment.

PRESENTATION OF RESULTS

The results of this study will be combined with the results of a subsequent study in the quality losses associated with weevil injury, and will be prepared for presentation as a Station Paper. In this paper the studies will be described, the results presented, and a method developed for determining the loss of volume and quality to be expected from weevil injury in individual white pine stands in the East.

SCHEDULE AND ASSIGNMENTS

Task	Completion Date	Man-Months
Work Plan	October, 1960	1
Conduct	November, 1960	2
Analysis and Publication	June, 1961	1